PENGUIN BOOKS

THE BLACK WOMAN'S GUIDE
TO FINANCIAL INDEPENDENCE

Cheryl D. Broussard has played the money game and won. Now she shares the secrets of her success with other Black women—and men—who want to become financially independent.

Cheryl knows the world of finance first hand. She started her career as a registered NYSE stockbroker and is currently a registered investment advisor and principal of Broussard & Douglas, Inc., a money management firm.

In addition to her practice, she lectures, writes, and conducts seminars throughout the country on money management and is the editor of "Invest in Yourself," a financial newsletter. Broussard lives in Oakland, California.

If you would like to receive additional information, including a sample of the "Invest in Yourself" newsletter, forthcoming seminars, and money management services, we can send you an information packet. Please write or call:

Broussard & Douglas, Inc.
499 Hamilton Ave., Suite 140
Palo Alto, CA 94301
Phone: (800)-488-0440
      (415)-688-1188
Fax: (415)-688-1166

THE BLACK WOMAN'S GUIDE TO FINANCIAL INDEPENDENCE

■ Smart Ways to Take Charge
of Your Money, Build Wealth,
and Achieve Financial Security

Cheryl D. Broussard

Registered Investment Advisor

PENGUIN BOOKS

PENGUIN BOOKS

Published by the Penguin Group

Penguin Books USA Inc., 375 Hudson Street, New York, New York 10014, U.S.A.

Penguin Books Ltd, 27 Wrights Lane, London W8 5TZ, England

Penguin Books Australia Ltd, Ringwood, Victoria, Australia

Penguin Books Canada Ltd, 10 Alcorn Avenue, Toronto, Ontario, Canada M4V 3B2

Penguin Books (N.Z.) Ltd, 182–190 Wairau Road, Auckland 10, New Zealand

Penguin Books Ltd, Registered Offices: Harmondsworth, Middlesex, England

First published in the United States of America by Hyde Park Publishing Co. 1991
This revised, updated edition published in Penguin Books 1996

10 9 8 7 6 5 4 3 2 1

PUBLISHER'S NOTE

This publication is designed to provide accurate and authoritative
information in regard to the subject matter covered. It is sold with the
understanding that the publisher is not engaged in rendering financial, legal,
or other professional service. If financial advice or other expert assistance is required,
the service of a competent professional person should be sought.

LIBRARY OF CONGRESS CATALOGING IN PUBLICATION DATA
Broussard, Cheryl D.
    The Black woman's guide to financial independence: smart ways to
  take charge of your money, build wealth, and achieve financial
  security/Cheryl D. Broussard.—Rev. and updated.
        p.   cm.
    Includes bibliographical references and index.
    ISBN 0 14 02.5283 5
    1. Afro-American women—Finance, Personal.   2. Investments.
  I. Title.
  HG179.B7463   1996
  332.024'042—dc20   95–36770

Printed in the United States of America
Set in Times New Roman
Designed by Victoria Hartman

*This book is dedicated
to my son, Hasan
and to the memory of
Barbara A. Clinton
and
Leonard C. Reid
who always told me to
"Never give up—you can do it"*

ACKNOWLEDGMENTS

This book could not have been written without many supportive people who provided their assistance and inspiration, among them: Shirley Jackson who assisted me in the typing of the manuscript; Jean Wiley and Mary Ellen Butler for their superb editing and suggestions; Valerie Irons, my publicist, who helped this book to become successful.

I thank the following for providing me with their expertise: Henry Cotten, Bronislaw Kuciak, Rosario Billingsley, Grace Douglas, Molly Duggan, Antoinette Broussard, Emma Pendergrass, Esq., Loraine Binion, Charlene R. Smith, C.P.A., and Brenda Wade, Ph.D.

Special appreciation goes to John Broussard; my mother and father, Gwendolyn J. Reid and Theodore Douglas; my grandparents, Leola and Hugh Clinton; and my mother-in-law, Maybelle Broussard; each one has given me the moral support to complete this book.

To my editor, Wendy Wolf, who believed in me from the beginning; and to my agents, Madeleine Morel and Barbara Lowenstein, thank you for your support and patience.

Finally, I wish to thank all black women because without you, there would not be a book.

CONTENTS

Contents

INTRODUCTION

The Black Woman's Guide to Financial Independence is an introduction to money management, written for all of the Black women I met throughout the country in my financial planning seminars who were desperately searching for answers to their financial problems. The book is addressed to all women, regardless of income, education, or work status, who have an interest in controlling their own financial destiny. It doesn't assume prior knowledge, education or experience in the financial world. But it does presume a willingness to learn and a strong determination to better your financial condition.

The Black Woman's Guide to Financial Independence will open your mind to the idea that **you can** achieve financial independence. It isn't a get-rich-quick book, but a book that will teach you to manage your financial life.

It isn't a book you read once and store in your bookcase until the new year rolls around and your new year's resolution is to this time **really** manage your money. Instead it's a workbook filled with worksheets that you should fill out as you go along. It's written in common sense language so you don't need a Ph.D. in finance to understand it.

Reading the book will demand much of your time and effort. However, if you are really interested in having control over your financial life—the time will be well spent.

There is nothing magical about the process of becoming financially independent. It doesn't require great luck or skill. But it does require knowledge, planning, discipline, and action.

No longer can African-American women afford to be consumer oriented. No longer can we afford to spend our money on material goods that don't generate money and prevent us from saving and developing an economic base.

We must also stop patronizing stores outside of the African-American community. By doing so, we are steadily giving away our economic power. Empowering the very people who are trying to keep us down.

The black dollar must turn over more than once in the African-American community if we are to rid our neighborhoods of the many social ills lurking about.

As black women we can play a large part in solving some of our social problems by learning about finance and business, taking care of our own money and then sharing the information with others in the African-American community.

The need for black women to understand and control their finances is a crucial issue for the 1990s. The statistics of black women and children living in poverty are startling. The media has erroneously given the perception that black women are achieving economic equality. This is far from the truth. Current statistics show that 45% of welfare recipients are single black females with sole support of their family. The income they receive is not even adequate for their basic level of living.

As black men are kept out of the work force, the rate of black women as head of household is rapidly increasing in the black community.

Black children today are three times more likely (than whites) to live in poverty. Black children in female-headed homes are 5 times more likely to live in poverty.

Black women who work full-time year-round earn 64 cents for every dollar a white male earns and 90 cents for every dollar earned by a white female. Which is why it is crucial that you learn what to do with the money that you do bring home instead of mismanaging it or giving it away to Uncle Sam.

Recent studies have shown that half of American marriages end in divorce, and it is the wife who suffers financially. It was found that a divorced husband's standard of living actually rose 42%, whlie that of his wife and children fell 73%.

According to the report, *Child Support and Alimony, 1985*, alimony and child support are paid to only 8% of black women who divorce versus 15.8% of white women. As a result, black women and children now make the largest percentage of America's new poor.

Even single black women cannot escape suddenly being cast into poverty. The $25,000-a-year single black woman who loses her job can suddenly become a member of the new poor if she doesn't have an emergency fund to cushion her.

Like so many of us, we are a job loss, illness, or divorce away from poverty—living paycheck to paycheck, not saving money for that untimely event.

The mismanagement of our money today will have an adverse financial effect during our retirement years.

Of the black women today who are over the age of 65, nearly 1 out of 5 are widows and live in poverty.

Many of the women haven't accumulated any assets and rely heavily on the federal government to subsidize them. Unfortunately, many of the women came from homes where they were unable to be a part of the financial decision making and as a result are financially in the dark.

The women also had jobs that did not provide retirement benefits. I'm sure that if they had understood money matters, they would have set aside something for their retirement years. No one in their right mind wants to live in poverty.

Although these statistics are depressing, it is information all black women need to know. And in spite of the fact that we are still subjected to racial and sexual discrimination in the workplace, which tends to limit our income and economic mobility, all is not lost, which is why this book is written especially for you. By obtaining knowledge and understanding economics and money you **can** beat the system. Opportunities still abound in America. They aren't readily visible, so you'll need to search hard for them. The purpose of this book is to guide you in the right direction to find those opportunities and to give you the confidence you will need to build a financial base.

The next decade is destined for black women to actively participate in business leadership. The time has come for you to control your own financial destiny. No longer can you afford to sit back and let others handle your money.

The Black Woman's Guide to Financial Independence is divided into 4 parts, each of which is crucial to developing a successful financial plan.

Part 1: Personal Money Management Strategies: In Chapter 1, I'll introduce you to 6 black women who have financial problems that are common to today's black women. I hope that by sharing their stories you will begin to focus on your financial condition and can avoid making future financial mistakes.

In Chapter 2, I discuss the significance of your habits and attitude toward money.

In Chapter 3, you will learn how important it is to have dreams and goals. Without them it will be very difficult for you to reach financial independence. When the going gets tough, your dreams and goals will keep you focused.

In Chapters 4, 5, 6, 7 and 8, you will learn how to get your financial life in order. Before you can begin a major financial overhaul, you will need to know where you currently stand. You also need to keep account of where your money is going. This can be accomplished by having a budget, knowing how to balance your checkbook, keeping track of how much you charge on credit cards, and keeping good financial records.

In Chapter 9, you'll learn the importance of teaching your children about the value of money and how to save and manage money, enabling them to become financial savvy adults later in life.

Part 2: Winning Tax and Savings Strategies: In Chapter 10, you will learn how to protect the assets you have worked so hard to accumulate. Without the proper insurance, your financial base could crumble after an unexpected death or emergency.

In Chapter 11, you will learn how to keep more of what you make by cutting your income taxes through strategic tax planning. Tax planning will enable you to have more discretionary income to use for your own savings that will help you to reach your goal of financial independence.

In Chapter 12, you will learn what to do with your savings money and how to maximize the return on your money.

Planning for your children's education is an important issue for the black family in the next century. In Chapter 13, you'll learn about the cost of education and ways to begin saving while your child is still young.

Modern medicine is allowing people to live much longer than ever before. If you want to live financially well during your leisure years it will take some serious planning. Chapter 14 will show you how to start planning and the type of investments that will increase your chances of having a retirement free of money worries.

Part 3: Investment Opportunities: The most exciting and lucrative part of your financial plan are the investments. Investing your money is the only way to substantially increase your net worth over time.

In Chapters 15 through 22, you'll learn about the stock and bond market, investing in international securities to take advantage of the new global economy and the advantages and disadvantages of investing in real estate.

Part 4: Putting It All Together: Making financial decisions is probably the most important job you have when your marriage ends. Yet this is such a stressful time, you're wondering how you can deal with such a task. In Chapter 23, "African-American Women, Money, and Divorce," you'll learn what financial steps you need to take to protect yourself during this time. If you're in the process of getting married for the first time or if you're remarrying, you may want to consider a prenuptial agreement. In this chapter you will learn if you're a prime candidate for a prenuptial agreement, and what you need to do to obtain one.

You'll also learn in this section that estate planning is necessary for everyone regardless of the amount of money you have. You will discover in Chapter 24 the advantages of having a will, what happens when you don't have one, and who can assist you in putting your estate plan together.

Chapter 25 will show you how to find and evaluate a financial advisor.

Chapter 26, Millionaire Power, puts it all together by summarizing the steps needed to master your financial future.

In the back of the book you'll find a complete glossary of terms used in personal finance and a resource section of books and organizations you can read and contact to help you to reach your goal of financial independence.

Throughout the book there are worksheets, tax tables, charts, and graphs. It is mandatory that you complete, review and update them monthly, quarterly, and yearly. If you don't have a savings account start one today. Always remember that nothing good happens to those who wait. Make something happen in your life by taking responsibility and action. Those are the keys to attaining your goal of financial independence. **GO FOR IT, TAKE ACTION NOW!**

Cheryl D. Broussard
Oakland, California

PART 1

PERSONAL MONEY MANAGEMENT STRATEGIES

CHAPTER 1

CASE STUDIES—
REAL WOMEN LIKE YOU

The following 6 stories are about real women just like you who came to my office seeking financial advice. For privacy purposes their names have been changed. In addition, their financial issues are not indicative of only one individual but are rather a compilation of all the women in a similar situation who sought my advice.

Each of the women have financial issues that are common among many women. Throughout the book I will advise on ways to solve financial problems similar to theirs.

Case 1
Single—Income over $35,000

Jean, 32, graduated 5 years ago from a top medical school and is now working for an HMO hospital in California. Currently, she earns $50,000 a year and presently has $5,000 saved in a 5½% bank savings account. Jean came to me because she has set a goal of buying a house within the next 2 years and wants to know how she can save more money for the down payment and

where she should invest her money to receive the highest return. In spite of the fact that she is single and making $50,000 a year, which is a lot of money for many women, she still feels she lives paycheck to paycheck and money seems to slip through her fingers. She wants to learn how to manage her money better.

She rents an apartment in Los Angeles for $1,000 a month and she just bought a new BMW. With insurance, her monthly car expense is $450.

Jean loves to shop and finds that she spends a lot of money on clothes and luxury items she doesn't necessarily need. She has 3 major credit cards and 5 department store charges, all of which are at their limits and charge a 19.2% finance charge. Her total amount of credit debt is $10,000. Every month she sends checks to these credit holders totaling $700.

Since Jean works many evenings, she eats out 4–5 times a week at a usual cost of $10–12 per evening.

Jean has a 401(k) matching retirement plan with her employer. Every month the company automatically takes 6% of her paycheck before taxes and for every dollar they match it with 50 cents. The money is placed in a growth-oriented mutual fund that she chose as her investment option. She started this plan when she first became employed and now has $7,000 saved. She also has a $2,000 IRA with a major bank.

Since the new tax laws went into effect, she has decided not to contribute to her IRA account.

Jean pays a substantial amount of her earnings to the government in taxes.

Case 2
Single—Income under $15,000

Linda, 27, works for a major savings and loan in Chicago as a bank teller. She has been with the bank for 5 years and wants to advance into banking management, so she is currently going to junior college in the evenings to work on her AA degree.

Linda's current income is $12,000 and in December she expects to receive a $500 bonus check. Linda already has plans for the money. She's been eyeing a $150 Louis Vuitton handbag and a $250 leather jacket since June, and plans to purchase both items the day she receives the money. She works hard and feels she deserves to buy these items.

Linda, like Jean, also feels she lives paycheck to paycheck. After paying her monthly basic needs and her monthly credit cards she has only a few dollars left over at the end of the month. Sometimes she doesn't have enough money to last her until the next pay period, so she obtains cash advances from her bank charge cards.

Linda has a savings account, but she has only $50 in her account. A couple of months ago she had $300 in her account, but had to use $250 of it to replace the brakes on her 1980 car. She's hoping nothing else will go wrong with her auto because she really can't afford to repair it, and she definitely cannot afford a new car.

Linda doesn't have any goals outside of wanting to advance at the bank. She figures she will marry soon and her husband will take care of her financially.

Case 3
Single with Children

Angela, 35, with 2 children, 13 and 15, was married to a very traditional man. Six months ago her husband, Steve, was laid off from his job and has not been able to find work. His unemployment has led to much pressure and strain in their relationship and Steve has decided to leave Angela and the children. Divorce papers have been filed and according to Angela's attorney, because Steve is unemployed he is not required to pay child support.

Angela married at the age of 20 and 2 years later had her first child. After graduating from high school she had worked briefly as a full-time receptionist for a company until she became pregnant. Being traditional, Steve wanted her to stay home with the children and he would be the breadwinner and handle all the finances. She agreed. Now because of her lack of employment experience she is unable to find full-time work.

After many months of no money coming in, Angela finally found a part-time job as a receptionist. She makes minimum wage of $4.25 per hour and works 25 hours a week. After taxes she brings home $80, a net annual figure of $4,160.

Since Steve moved out, Angela has been paying the bills, something she has never done before. Last month she received 3 overdrawn slips from her bank. She doesn't understand how to balance the checkbook and she is too afraid to ask for assistance because she doesn't want to appear ignorant.

Angela is very concerned about her children. They both attend public schools, but she can barely afford to clothe and feed them. Every night she prays that her children will not become ill, because since Steve lost his job, they no longer have a medical plan. And with her salary she cannot afford medical bills. Angela cannot understand how she let herself get into this predicament.

Case 4
Married with Children

Elizabeth, 45, has 3 children. One is a freshman in a private college and is hoping to attend medical school 4 years from now. The other 2 are in their third and fourth year of high school. Elizabeth earns $25,000 as a teacher and has been with the school system for 25 years and plans to retire in 10 years at the age of 55. Elizabeth's husband, Jim, earns $35,000 and is a supervisor for the U.S. Post Office. He has worked for the government for 30 years and works part-time in his present sideline business of real estate investments.

Elizabeth and Jim own 2 apartment buildings in addition to their home. One of the units is occupied by Elizabeth's mother who is 75 years old. Their home is almost paid off and when Jim retires they plan to purchase additional pieces of property.

Elizabeth has 3 concerns about her finances. 1) All of their money seems to be tied up in real estate. She is concerned that they are real estate rich and cash poor. 2) Although Elizabeth really wants to retire in 10 years; she wants to make sure she is still able to afford the life-style she is accustomed to. She has a TSA (tax sheltered annuity) but it might not be enough. 3) Soon her children will be in college and one in medical school. She has read in many financial magazines that in the next decade college cost will triple and there will not be as many scholarships available. How will she pay for her children's education?

Case 5
Retired—Married

Alice is 60 years old and next month she and John will celebrate their forty-fifth wedding anniversary. They have worked very hard

5

and now they want to enjoy life more. They are both retired and would like to spend most of their time traveling throughout the United States and abroad.

They have sacrificed quite a bit while working and have a nice size nest egg of $300,000. They feel that the interest from their nest egg along with their social security and pension checks should be enough to live comfortably. Alice is **ultra** conservative regarding her finances. Currently the $300,000 is in 3 fixed rate certificates of deposit at their local bank. She grew up during the depression years and feels her money is safer in the banks.

She is also a penny pincher; her philosophy is, *if I don't have the cash*, then I don't buy it. She has a couple of bank credit cards, but will only use them when necessary and once the bill arrives, she pays it off within 30 days to avoid the finance charge.

Alice has a beautiful home which is completely paid for, and property taxes are low. Alice's overall financial condition looks good. But Alice has 2 major financial problems: 1) Alice pays too much in taxes because she has no exemptions or deductions, and 2) the value of her money is not growing and keeping pace with inflation since all of her money is invested in fixed rate certificates of deposit, resulting in the loss of her buying power.

Case 6
Retired—Widowed

Alana D., 73, has been a widow for the last 5 years and is struggling financially. Her husband did not believe in life insurance, so when he died, Alana did not receive any money. It took practically all of her life savings to pay for the burial. Alana was very young when she married. She and Mr. D. lived in the south. When they married Mr. D.'s family gave him 25 acres of farm land. But during that time everyone was moving to the city, so Alana and Mr. D. followed, leaving the land behind.

Alana and Mr. D. have had several offers on the land throughout the years but Mr. D. never wanted to sell. When Mr. D. died Alana was offered a substantial amount for the property and she was very willing to sell, except there was one major problem. Mr. D. did not leave a will and the property was held only in his name, not joint with right of survivorship. This caused a tremendous problem for Alana, which prevented her from selling the land immediately. It is now 5 years later, and Alana is still fighting with the courts over the land.

Alana receives $450 a month from social security and an additional $75 from her husband's pension. Alana has never worked. Also she does not have children and therefore cannot depend on anyone else financially.

In a low income housing complex, in not one of the best neighborhoods in town, she pays $275 for rent. This leaves her with $250 a month on which to live. Within the last 6 months coming home from the grocery store, she has been robbed twice.

Alana is not in the best of health and does not have medical insurance, she depends on Medicare. Alana is very angry with herself because of the financial straits she is in. If only she had put aside some of her allowance money in a separate account, she could have saved a lot of money. And if only she had insisted on life insurance and having a will she would be better off financially.

CHAPTER 2

MONEY ATTITUDES & HABITS

As young children many black women were told by their parents that money is the root of all evil. They were told not to worry about money matters because that was the responsibility of the man of the house. Unfortunately many of us today still believe these sayings to be true. Black women have not overcome years of childhood conditioning. Our money habits have derived from the cultural and religious attitude and habits of our parents. This upbringing has predetermined the way we invest, save and squander our money.

Many of our parents were unable to save and invest their money. They were too busy trying to provide food and clothes for the family on the low income they received. As a result, with limited knowledge and opportunities for our parents to make money, black women and men were not taught good money management habits. According to marketing studies on black individual spending habits, blacks save less than 4% of their money and are greater spenders than the general population. We hold less than 1% of interest-earning financial investments such as stocks, bonds, mutual funds and money market accounts. But over 10% of our money is tied up in automobiles, expensive clothing and other consumable items that don't pay interest and are discarded within a short time. These are the consumption habits that play a large part in the demise of the economic status of the black family and continue the poverty cycle throughout the community. This money should instead be used to create jobs and businesses in the African-American communities.

Black women must distance themselves from this consumerism mentality. We need to develop saving habits and forgo buying the $300 designer handbags and invest the money in an account that will earn interest and build into something for the future. Once you have developed a savings plan and reached a level where you have a large sum of money ($25,000–30,000) in an investment account, by all means buy the handbag because you deserve it.

Another negative money management habit found among women is the tendency to overcharge on credit cards. Credit cards should be used only for emergency or 30-day convenient purchases. Credit card management will be discussed further in a later chapter.

The best habit to a healthy money management program and financial security is to stick to a budget and curb your spending.

Attitude

Having a PMA (positive mental attitude) is necessary to create wealth.

Your attitude about money has a tremendous effect on how you value and spend money. People who are wealthy aren't smarter than you, they just have a positive attitude toward money and an understanding of how to use money to their advantage. You can easily do this too.

Having a positive mental attitude and a **"Can Do"** spirit increases your chances of obtaining wealth and financial independence. There is a lot of negativity in the world today. The media as well as our family and friends are forever focusing on the negatives. Don't let others influence your life and make it miserable. Don't blame your financial circumstances on the government, the economy, or your parents. That's the easy way out, and it prevents you from moving ahead.

Stop making excuses. Always be up about life, have a positive mental attitude, take responsibility for your own financial welfare and take action. Just the fact of reading this book shows you want more control over your financial life and are willing to make changes that will lead to financial independence.

You must be willing to change your attitude and totally commit yourself to become a financial success. You shape your own financial life by the attitude you hold each day. If you have a poor attitude about studying money management, you will not learn very much until you change that attitude. If you have an attitude of failure you are defeated before you start. You must set out with the attitude that you can accomplish whatever you set out to do.

■ **NOTES**

_____

_____

_____

_____

_____

CHAPTER 3

DREAMS & GOALS

Where Do You Want to Go?

Dreams

There is a famous saying by William James, *"Anything the mind can believe and conceive it can achieve."* The key to becoming financially independent is knowing where you want to go. You can begin by dreaming and setting financial goals for yourself. Your dreams are one of your most powerful tools for success.

Take the time to dream big and plan out your success. You'll be amazed at how many of your dreams you can actualize. Too many of us are content to drift from day to day without any definite goals or plans. We spend more time planning our two week vacation than we do our finances. If you follow this path, you, too, will become a victim of circumstance. You will be pushed this way and that by events which you seem to have no control over. You will be subject to the opinions and actions of others. Don't forget, you have the power of choice and if you want to succeed you must know clearly and precisely what you want.

Every day visualize yourself achieving the goals you have set out to accomplish. Visualize yourself paying off your credit card debt or starting a business. See yourself with $25,000 or $100,000 in your savings account. These are the dreams and visions which motivate you to save money instead of spending it.

Goals

Your goals are the stepping stones toward the achievement of your dreams. They are the experiences you have not had, places you have not been, and money you have not received. There is no limit to the amount of goals you can have. In fact, you should have as many goals as you can imagine. Many of us are so accustomed to not having what we want that we place limitations on ourselves.

Your goals are important because they design and direct your life and assist you in experiencing the excitement, joy, and happiness that you deserve. Without goals, you will find yourself living from problem to problem instead of from opportunity to opportunity; you will allow other people and daily pressures to control you.

If you are unsure how to define your goals, begin by asking yourself questions such as: What would you like to have? What would you like to do? Where would you like to go? And what would you like to give back to society? An example of financial goals you might want to focus on are 1) buying your first home, 2) sending your children to college, and 3) saving for your retirement. But your number one priority goal is financial independence; for with this you enter into the world of economic empowerment.

Having money brings flexibility and freedom into your life. You can work as long as it pleases you and in an area you choose because it is emotionally and spiritually fulfilling.

The first step is to write out your goals on 3 levels. The first level is short term goals, those you want to accomplish within 1 year, e.g., paying off your credit cards. Second is intermediate goals, those you want to accomplish in 3 to 5 years, e.g., buying a home or car. And the third is long term goals, ones that take 5 years or longer to achieve, e.g., your children's education and saving for your retirement. **Worksheet 3-1** will aid you in writing down your goals.

It is also important that you are specific and state a time and the amount of money it will take to achieve your goals. Writing down these financial goals and setting a time limit will cause you to focus daily on what you need to do to reach them.

Your financial goals are not written in stone and can be changed as your life-style changes. Read your goals at least every other day and begin right now to act on them. Time is of the essence. Achieving your goals takes patience and a long-term view. By planning you are making a commitment to take charge of your financial life.

Goals and Dreams

Dream/Goal	Date to accomplish	Dollars Needed
Financially Independent		
Build an Emergency Cash Fund		
Reduce Credit Card Debt		
Buy a House		
Increase Insurance Coverage		
Finance Children's Education		
Take Early Retirement		
Make a Large Purchase: • Car • Vacation • Real Estate • Other		
Start a Business		
Start a Family		
Other _____ _____ _____ _____ _____		

1) Age you desire to be financially independent _____

2) They type of life-style you desire at retirement or when you become financially independent and no longer need to work for income _____

_____

_____

_____

Worksheet 3-1 Goals and Dreams

CHAPTER 4

CURRENT FINANCIAL STANDING

Where Are You Today?

Now that you know what you want, the next step is to find out where you currently stand financially and what assets you have for developing a strategy to reach your goals.

Your first step is to calculate a net-worth statement which is also called a personal balance sheet. See **Worksheet 4-1**. A net-worth statement lists all your financial assets and liabilities. It is an inventory of everything you own that has a dollar value.

Your net-worth statement can supply you with loads of important information such as how much debt you have, whether it is too much, and whether or not you are accumulating enough assets to support yourself during retirement. Completing your net-worth statement is an essential step for developing a sound investment strategy to assist you on the road to financial independence. It should be completed annually.

Your net-worth statement will serve many purposes particularly when you are purchasing real estate or trying to qualify for a loan. The first form banks and savings and loans require is a net-worth statement. Therefore it is to your advantage to understand in detail how to complete your net-worth statement.

The financial assets on your net-worth statement include your home, car, cash, investments, IRA and pension account, investment real estate, cash value of life insurance policies and personal items. You must use the current market value of these items.

The value of your investments and insurance policies can be obtained from your banker, broker or insurance agent. Your company should be able to tell you what your pension benefits are worth. To obtain the current market value of your home and investment real estate, talk to your real estate agent. You can get an estimate of your car's worth by consulting the Blue Book, a guide published by the National Automobile Dealers Association which lists the current value of used cars.

Your personal items may require more research. Compare your items with current items that are on the market today. Remember that your items are used and will not resale at the full price, you must use sound judgment when pricing.

Next, compute your total financial liabilities (money you owe). These include the mortgage on your home, credit card balances, income taxes, car loans, college loans and any other debt obligations.

After you have completed both sides, deduct your liabilities from your assets and the result is what you are currently worth. Your financial objective is to increase your net worth annually. This can be accomplished in 2 ways: 1), by lowering the amount of your liabilities and 2), increasing your assets, which we will cover in later chapters.

■ **NOTES**

_____

_____

_____

_____

_____

_____

_____

_____

_____

_____

_____

_____

_____

_____

_____

_____

Net-Worth Statement

Assets (Has cash value)		Liabilities (Your Debts)	
Liquid Assets		**Current Debts**	
Cash and Checking Account	$_____	Rent/Mortgage	$_____
Money Market Account	$_____	Charge Accounts	$_____
CDs and Savings Account	$_____	Insurance Premiums	$_____
Stocks and Mutual Funds	$_____	Education	$_____
Bonds	$_____	Other	$_____
Cash Surrender Value Life Insurance	$_____	Total	$_____
Other	$_____		
Total Liquidation Assets	$_____	**Taxes**	
		Federal	$_____
Investment Assets		State	$_____
Real Estate	$_____	Property Taxes	$_____
IRA/Keogh	$_____	Social Security	$_____
Business Ownership Interest	$_____	Total	$_____
Annuities	$_____		
Notes Receivable (*money owed to you*)	$_____	**Other Loans**	
Collectibles	$_____	Auto	$_____
Tax Shelters	$_____	Education	$_____
Vested Pension	$_____	Life Insurance	$_____
Home Mortgage	$_____	Home Improvement	$_____
Total Investment Assets	$_____	Other	$_____
		Total	$_____
Personal Assets			
Home	$_____		
Automobile	$_____		
Clothing/Jewelry etc.	$_____	**Net Worth**	
Household Goods	$_____	Total Assets	$_____
Other	$_____	Total Liabilities	−$_____
Total Assets	$_____	Net Worth	$_____

Worksheet 4-1 Net-Worth Statement

CHAPTER 5

FINANCIAL RECORDKEEPING

Where You Are Today

A good record-keeping system is an important part of your financial plan. Getting organized financially is well worth the time and effort. It provides you with a more accurate view of your financial condition, and helps to pinpoint any potential problems.

Keeping complete records is an effective money management tool. It can help to document deductible expenses, thus, save you taxes and can provide you with evidence in case of a tax audit.

Your record keeping can be a simple file system. Certain important papers and records should be kept in a safe deposit box in a bank and others in a safe file at home.

Figure 5-1 provides a sample of important documents and the length of time you need to keep them.

The following papers are difficult to replace and should be kept in a safe deposit box:

- Birth certificates
- Stock and bond certificates
- Real estate deeds, mortgage records, home improvement receipts
- Marriage certificates
- Title to your automobile
- Passports
- Contracts
- Copy of your will
- Citizenship papers
- Small business papers
- Death certificates
- Military service papers
- Adoption papers
- Household inventory with photographs

Do not place your life insurance policies and the original copy of your will into the safe deposit box because in many states when the owner or joint owner of a safe deposit box dies, the bank seals the box until all tax and legal matters are taken care of. The sealing prevents the surrender of your insurance policy and the insurance company will not pay until the policy is surrendered. Also, the court cannot probate your will until the last will is presented. The best place to keep your life insurance policies is at

Keeping Important Documents

Documents	Where To Store	How Long
Birth Certificate, Marriage Certificate	Original—Safe Deposit Box Copy—Home File Box	Indefinitely
Loan Agreements	Home File Box	Until Paid Off
Passport	Home File Box	Renew Every 10 Years
Will	Attorney or Safe Deposit Box	Indefinitely
Trust Documents	Attorney and Safe Deposit Box	Indefinitely
Stock and Bond Certificates	Broker or Safe Deposit Box	Until Sold
Automobile Title	Safe Deposit Box	Until Sold
Insurance Policies	Safe Deposit Box and Home File Box	Indefinitely
Net Worth Statement	Home File Box	Update Annually
Savings Account Passbook	Home File Box	Indefinitely
Certificate of Deposit	Home File Box	Indefinitely
Tax Returns/Supporting Paperwork	Home File Box	3 to 7 Years
Mortgage Records	Safe Deposit Box	Until Property Sold
Real Estate deeds	Safe Deposit Box	Until Property Sold
Property Title	Safe Deposit Box	Until Property Sold
Bills	Home File Box	1 Year
Cancelled Checks/Bank Statements	Home File Box	10 Years
Credit Card Numbers	Home File Box	Keep Current

Figure 5-1 Record Keeping

home and your will in the files of your attorney.

Records that should be kept at home safely, whether in a file cabinet or a shoe box include:

- Automobile insurance policies
- Bank books and statements
- Income tax returns

- Homeowner insurance
- Life insurance policies
- Investment papers of stock and bond transactions
- Bills: 1 year current file; 2–5 years for bills needed for evidence for tax purposes
- Property tax records
- Will (copy of original)
- Household inventory (copy)

CHAPTER 6

CASH MANAGEMENT

Budgeting—Keeping Track of Your Expenses

It's the second of the month and you were just paid on the thirty-first of the preceding month. Do you find yourself asking where oh where has my money gone? Join the crowd, 90% of working people in America are still living paycheck to paycheck every month. It affects many regardless of their income level. It's a symptom—not of lack of income but of a cash flow problem. And the cure is having a budget.

Having a budget is a key ingredient to proper money management. Its purpose is to show you where you need to control and decrease your expenses. It also tells you the amount of discretionary income you have or don't have available for savings and investment purposes. It can quickly show you the reason why you have more than monthly income.

Prepare your cash management statement by month for the complete year and review it monthly. Compare whether or not you stayed within the amount you budgeted for in each category. This will tell you where you need to cut down.

Now, I know you are probably saying "I don't have time to fill this out every month." Yes, I know you never have enough time. But if your objective is to reach financial independence and some of the other goals you've set for yourself, this step cannot be overlooked. Following a budget is just like dieting, it takes a lot of discipline. But the rewards are well worth the extra effort.

The first step in developing a budget is to list all sources of income. See **Worksheet 6-1**. On this sheet list all your income for yourself and spouse. Include money from salary, extra money from a part-time job or hobbies, interest from savings accounts, dividends from investments, rent from property you own, and social security or pension payments.

The second step is to list all your expenses. This area consists of 2 categories, fixed and non-fixed. Fixed expenses are those which do not change. They include rent, mortgage payment, insurance payment, taxes, and automobile payments. They are consistent monthly payments.

Non-fixed expenses are those which you do have some control over. They are payments that vary in amount, monthly. These include food, clothing, entertainment and recreation, magazine subscriptions, credit card payments and many other miscellaneous items. In this categroy most of your unnecessary expenses can be reduced or eliminated. A particular area is credit card debt. Black women pay 40% of their income to charge card payments (more on credit cards in a later chapter).

The second area of high expenses is the miscellaneous column which includes magazine subscriptions, entertainment, dinners out, hairdressing salon, clothes and cosmetics. Before you spend money in these areas ask yourself whether you really have to have it. Most of the time the answer is no. Asking yourself this question before you make that purchase puts a clamp on overspending.

In the fixed category an area that is habitually overlooked is the savings column. This most important expense is the toughest to make. It should be used as an emergency fund and should contain from 3 to 6 months of net (with taxes taken out) monthly income. It is cash intended for emergencies only, and emergencies do not include the $300 blue suede shoes you *must* have, but do include a major auto repair or a period of unemployment. Yes, this area takes a lot of discipline. The key to starting and maintaining this account is to pay yourself first. Ideally you should save 10% of your net monthly income, but at first this may be too high, so I suggest you start with 5% and work your way up to 10% or more.

After you have maintained your budget for 3–4 months, you will begin to notice a change in your attitude toward spending. Many of you who thought you didn't have

money for savings will be amazed at the amount you have been wasting on items you really didn't need and could have placed in an interest bearing account.

After you have completed filling out all sections of your budget, subtract your expenses from your income. If you find that the final figure is negative, you have what is known as deficit spending; in other words you spend more money than you make monthly and you need to go on a serious spending diet.

Don't look upon your budget as something you dread doing every month. Look at it in a positive way as a step that will lead you closer to obtaining financial independence. Your financial fitness can only be achieved by being aware of your spending habits and knowing where your money is going. Remember, in order for this system to work you have to stick to it. Don't expect miracles to happen overnight and don't be inflexible; your budget is not engraved in stone. Lifestyles do change. Change your budget along with it and review it monthly, quarterly, and annually to track your progress.

Some suggested spending ranges as a percentage of your net income are:

Housing	25%
Food	15%
Utilities	10%
Clothing	5%
Savings	10%
Child Care	8–10%
Entertainment & Recreation	10%
Miscellaneous	5–7%

Money Management 101

Monthly Income: $_____
Investment Income: $_____

Monthly Income: $_____
Investment Income: $_____

Expenses	Budgeted	Actual	Expenses	Budgeted	Actual
FOOD			**INVESTMENTS**		
Groceries			Securities		
Lunch			Real Estate		
Restaurant			Retirement Account		
HOUSING			Other		
Mortgage/Rent			**AUTOMOTIVE**		
Electricity			Payment/Leases		
Gas/Oil			Gas/Oil		
Taxes			Insurance		
Insurance			License/Registration		
Water/Sewer			Maintenance/Repairs		
Telephone			Other		
Repairs/Maintenance			**ENTERTAINMENT/RECREATION**		
Other			Children's Activities		
CLOTHING			Weekend Trips		
Work Attire			Family/Friend Activities		
Leisure & Sports			Vacations		
Children's			Other		
Laundry/Cleaning			**MISCELLANEOUS**		
Other			Toiletries/Cosmetics		
TAXES			Beauty/Barber		
Income Taxes			Petty Spending Cash		
Social Security Tax			Allowances		
Other			Gifts (Christmas)		
SAVINGS			Newspaper		
Emergency Fund			Periodicals		
Other			Dues (Union, Clubs, etc.)		
INSURANCE			ATM		
Medical			Credit Cards		
Disability			Other		
Life					
Other					
MEDICAL					
Doctor/Dentist			**TOTAL EXPENSES**		
Medicine/Drugs			Discretionary Income		
Other					

Worksheet 6-1 Money Management

CHAPTER 7

BALANCING YOUR CHECKBOOK

Understanding how to balance your checkbook is another way of managing your cash flow. Your checking account can help you keep a record of your income and expenses. When you balance your checkbook you can see exactly where the money is going and in what area you need to adjust your spending. This information is very helpful at tax time and in case of an audit by the I.R.S. A properly managed checking account can also be an excellent credit reference. It will show how you handle your finances.

Your checking account recordkeeping should be simple and consistent. Every time you write a check or deposit money record it immediately in the check register—the booklet provided to you by the bank. A sample of the checkbook register is provided on **Worksheet 7-1**.

It is particularly important to keep track of electronic fund transfers. These are deposits or withdrawals made at an automated teller machine or merchandise you buy from a grocery store or retailer that allows you to pay for it by using your card to debit your checking account. It's easy to forget these transactions.

Every month when you receive your bank statement review and compare your check amounts, withdrawals, deposits and ATM transactions with the check register. Banks and computers do make mistakes. If you find a mistake contact your bank.

Unless you balance your checkbook regularly you'll never know how much money you have in your account. If you write a check without enough money to cover it, it will bounce. This will entail paying a fee to the bank, which can range from $10–$20 per check and a fee from the business that allowed you to write the check. That fee can range from 3 times the amount of purchase to $100.

Don't plan on using float to cover a check you have written with a deposit. (A float is the time it takes the checks to reach the bank where it will be paid.) Computers have now made this much more difficult. A check you write today could be cashed and subtracted from your account later that same day. So if you know you don't have enough money to cover, don't write the check. The chances of it bouncing are very high.

Bringing Your Records Up-to-Date

If you haven't balanced your checkbook for several months, there are several steps you can take today to bring your records up-to-date:

- Gather all of your records of deposits, withdrawals, and checks written.
- Gather your last 12 months of bank statements. If you can't locate them contact your bank, they can provide you with a copy for a small charge.
- Start with the oldest statement and balance your checkbook one statement at a time.
- Make sure you subtract or add all withdrawals and deposits and other bank fees that are easily overlooked.
- Check off each check and verify the amount.
- Compare the ending balance in your check register with the bank statement. If you find a big difference, areas of possible errors that you should double check are:
  - Arithmetic
  - Transposing of numbers
  - Missed recording of transactions
  - Missing checks
  - Deposit amounts are different from the bank
  - Incorrect carrying forward of the balance in the check register.
  - Missed ATM or other electronic fund Transactions (EFT).

After going through this list if you still aren't balancing, gather all your statements, checkbook, and ATM transactions and visit your bank for assistance. Your bank may charge a fee for this service.

Once you've balanced your checkbook continue to keep it up-to-date so you will know how much money you have in your checking account from day to day.

High-Tech Money Management

If you own a computer, balancing your checkbook and managing your money is now much easier with the use of financial software programs. They are powerful and easy to use. You can use them to keep track of all your financial transactions, no matter how simple or complex, for home or business, or for both.

With the more popular programs such as Quicken and Kiplinger's Simply Money, you can print checks, balance your accounts, keep track of your credit card debt, set up a budget for your income and expenses, monitor your investment portfolio, and try out "what if" scenarios for loan planning, retirement planning, and money management.

Using the computer to manage your finances will save you an inordinate amount of time and money, especially at tax time.

If you have a modem, there is now a convenient way to pay your bills electronically with a service called Checkfree that is available through most of the computer banking programs. You simply have your modem dial Checkfree and indicate what bills you want paid. The company either pays the bill electronically or prints and mails a check. There is a cost involved, but it is nominal compared to the time and effort it takes to write out the checks, buy stamps, and mail them. A listing of money management software programs is available in the resources section.

■ NOTES

_____

_____

_____

_____

_____

_____

_____

_____

_____

_____

_____

_____

_____

Check Register

Record transactions below. Checks, Express Stop Withdrawals, Express Transfers, and Deposits.

CHECK NO.	DATE	TRANSACTIONS	TAX DEDUCT CODES	TRANSACTION AMOUNT	✓	DEPOSIT AMOUNT	BALANCE
							100.00
101	8/2	ABC Grocery		25 92			-25.92
		Food					74.08
	8/5	Deposit				250.00	+250.00
		Paycheck					324.08
ATM	8/5	Cash Withdraw		40 00			-40.00
							284.08
	8/10	Checking Acct Fee		6 00			-6.00
							278.08

Figure 7-1 Check Register

CHAPTER 8

CREDIT CARD MANAGEMENT

Getting Out of Debt

After completing the cash flow **Worksheet 6-1** did you find that once you subtracted your expenses from your income you had a negative result? If you did, the most likely reason for it was because of your credit card debt, and you are living beyond your means. Credit card debt is one of the major reasons many women are far from financial independence. We live in a credit based society where women are considered the major consumers. We are daily enticed with advertisements encouraging us to spend our money, and as a result we have become a nation of creditaholics. That's where the trouble begins.

There is much competition among financial institutions to sign up people for credit cards. If you have at least one card and have paid on it fairly regularly, you will most likely receive numerous unsolicited direct mail pieces offering credit with initial low finance charges or waiver of the first year annual fee. Beware, there is always a catch. Be sure to read the fine print before you sign on.

Credit cards are an excellent source of short-term interest-free credit and an invaluable source of emergency cash. They should be used for safety and convenience, not borrowing. Unfortunately, many women like Jean, use and abuse their credit to the point of financial trouble. You have to remember that although credit cards are plastic, the bills must be repaid with real dollars. Credit cards are loans with enormous amounts of interest charged. It isn't free money, although the advertisements will have you believe it is, with their "just charge it" philosophy.

Cost of Credit

There are 2 major costs to having credit cards: 1) the annual fee, and 2) the finance charges. The annual fees for major credit cards range from $12 to $55. To entice you to sign up for credit, many credit card companies waive the first year fee. After that you're hooked and you'll have to pay the annual fee if you have an outstanding balance.

Credit card finance charges vary from 15 to 23% depending on the state of the credit operation. Some banks offer floating rates which are tied to the Prime rate, the advantage being a rate much lower then the average credit card interest rate of 19.2%, even during periods of high interest rates. **Figure 8-1** shows how much a credit card can cost per year in finance charges.

You can see that by adding finance charges and fees to your purchases made on credit, the advantage of buying what you want now is a lot more expensive. There are banks and credit card companies that offer lower fees and finance charges. Shop around. *Bankcard Holders of America*, a nonprofit credit card awareness organization, has compiled a list of banks with low finance charges and low or no annual fees. To receive the list send $4 to: Bankcard Holders of America, 524 Branch Drive, Salem, VA 24153.

How to Start Credit

As mentioned earlier, this is a credit based society and in order to become financially independent it is necessary to establish a healthy credit history. The problem many black women face is that banks will not give them credit unless they already have credit. So the question you ask is how do I get started?

The first step is to open a savings account in your name. If you have been banking at a particular bank for some time, start there. Apply for a small personal loan, using your savings account as collateral. Pay off the loan in monthly installments and make sure you get the payment in way ahead of the due date.

If you are married, when you and your husband apply for credit, advise the bank or store to which you apply that when they receive a credit report request, the report should be in your name as well as your husband's. Be sure to apply in your full name, i.e., Mary Doe, not Mrs. John Doe. If you are recently divorced, you can still apply for credit based on the accounts you held with your husband.

If you ever want to check your credit history there are credit rating agencies with offices throughout the United States. You can obtain a copy of your credit file by written request. There is usually a charge of $8 to $10, unless you have been turned down by a creditor; then it is free. Contact the following headquarters of the major national credit rating agencies, or check the yellow pages for offices in your area.

TRW
505 City Park Way West
Orange, CA 92668
(714) 385-7000

Credit Rating Bureau, Inc.
P.O. Box 95007
Atlanta, GA 30347
(404) 252-9559

Cost of Credit Cards

Amount Charged Interest Rate (19.2%)	$25.00	$50.00	$100.00	$500.00	$1000.00	$5000.00
	+	+	+	+	+	+
Interest Cost	4.75	9.50	19.00	95.00	190.00	950.00
Total Cost Purchase	$29.75	$59.50	$119.00	$595.00	$1190.00	$5950.00

Figure 8-1 Cost of Credit Cards

Credit Card Management

Credit cards offer many benefits. They allow you to purchase and do things that you might never be able to do or get. But remember: either credit controls you or you control credit. If you are interested in becoming financially independent (which I hope you are, since you bought this book) you should pick the latter.

The best way to manage credit cards is to pay the full balance each month. Most credit cards have a grace period of 25 to 30 days between the date you are billed and a finance charge. You can use this to your advantage by making a purchase right after the billing date listed on your statement to delay being billed for this purchase for almost 2 months. If you pay in full when you receive the bill, you have profited from the free credit for those 2 months.

Obtain a travel and expense credit card such as American Express or Diners Club.

When purchases are charged on these cards the balance must be paid in full every month. Knowing this, you are much more likely to stop and reconsider before you purchase.

How Much Is Too Much Credit?

Budgeting is just as important to credit cards as it is to cash. The total of your monthly credit card payments should not exceed 15 to 20% of your take home pay. This is known as your debt ratio **(Figure 8-2)**, and you can calculate this figure by obtaining the numbers from your budget **Worksheet 6-1**. If you find that your percentage is higher than 20%, you are most likely robbing Peter to pay Paul, and borrowing to meet your daily expenses. If you are finding yourself in this predicament it's time to kick the spending habit. Unfortunately, this isn't easy. But the best way is cold turkey. Yes it will be tough, but you can do it. Place your credit cards in a friend's safety deposit box, or as a last resort, cut them in half and return to the issuers with a letter of explanation. Look over your budget and cut out all expenses that don't meet your basic necessities. Place this money in an account earmarked for credit card reduction only. Double up on payments where possible. You must put yourself on this strict regimen to achieve personal financial independence.

If you question your willpower and find you cannot stick to a credit card budget, then obtain the advice of a credit card counselor who will assist you with planning a budget to liquidate your debts. There are many agencies listed in your yellow pages. Beware, some charge exorbitant fees. The best agency is the *National Foundation for Consumer Credit*—a nonprofit debt counseling service. They will plan a budget and make a list of all debts and then contact your creditors to arrange a payoff schedule. There is a nominal fee of 6½% with a maximum of $20 per month for postage and paperwork. Look in the yellow pages for a member agency of the National Foundation of Consumer Credit. If you can't find one, write to the Foundation at 8710 George Ave., Silver Springs, MD 20910.

Avoid checking accounts with overdraft protection. They allow your checking account balance to go into the red. You are essentially taking out a loan every time you use it. This can be **DANGEROUS**.

Smart Debt Strategies

The uncertain economic climate calls for black women to drastically reduce their debt burden. This can be done with several easily executed strategies. Follow these, and they'll keep you out of trouble.

Strategy 1: Leave home without your credit cards. If they're too accessible the likelihood of your using them is high. If you find youself in line ready to pull out your card, take a moment to ask yourself, would I buy this if I were paying cash? You may also want to consider putting the item on hold until the next day. This will give you time to really think about the purchase.

Strategy 2. Most of us get in trouble with overspending when we're feeling down or we've had a bad day at work. When you feel the urge to shop, go work out or take a walk instead. You'll get the same euphoric feeling that shopping gives you.

Strategy 3: If you're already saddled with credit card balances, you can speed up the process of digging yourself out by avoiding the "minimum-payment syndrome." Send in a few dollars more than your minimum monthly payment. By adding just $10 more than the minimum due each month, a woman with a $3,300 balance will pay off the debt in four years instead of nineteen and save over $2,500 in interest.

Strategy 4: Develop a systematic plan to pay off your credit cards. Pay off the debt in order of the highest interest rate first. If you're unsure how to develop a payment plan there is a debt management program called the Debt Zapper developed by Bankcard Holders of America. You provide the agency with information on your outstanding credit card balances, interest rates, and the minimum amount due, and they will provide you with a computer generated month-by-month schedule that spells out exactly how much you should pay on each card every month, with the largest amount going to the cards with the highest interest rates.

Strategy 5: Refinance your existing credit cards. There's no reason to pay 19.2% when the competition is offering cards with single-digit rates and no annual fees. Shop around for a lower rate card and then call your card issuer and ask them to lower your rate. If you're a customer in good standing they probably will because they don't want to lose your account. If they don't, consider changing to a different card.

Strategy 6: Don't use your credit card for anything that will be gone by the time the monthly statement comes—groceries, meals, movie tickets—unless you always pay off your balance each month. Imagine paying for 1 night out on the town or a carload of groceries over 2 to 3 years. This is definitely *not* smart money management.

Home Equity/Consolidation Loans— Should I Use Them to Pay Off My Credit Card Debt?

Extreme caution is needed when considering paying off your debt with a consolidation or home equity loan. These loans offer the convenience of one-stop payments but there is a catch. These loans cost you more money because they are stretched out anywhere from 10 to 20 years, which increases the amount of your interest expense. With the home equity loan you gain the benefits of tax deductibility on the interest, but you trade unsecured debt for secured debt, thereby putting your home at risk.

The major problem with these types of loans is that once you begin to feel comfortable with your new low payment, you may resume charging and reopening lines of credit that you had previously paid off with the loan. Then it's "deja debt" all over again.

I recommend avoiding these loans if at all possible. Instead get yourself on a payment plan and stick to it.

Bankruptcy—The Last Resort

In 1978, Congress passed the Bankruptcy Reform Act, Chapter 13, known as the "Wage Earner Plan" and Chapter F which is a straight bankruptcy. Chapter 13 allows you to consolidate debts and repay a court-approved percentage over 3 years. The creditors must postpone interest and late charges and cannot continue to send you dunning letters.

Chapter F is the real thing—voluntary personal bankruptcy. This wipes out your debt and the court will collect, sell and distribute your assets. Bankruptcy proceedings should only be used as the last resort. Remember to contact an attorney before filing.

Calculating Your Personal Debt Ratio

	Monthly	Annually
1. Your Total Take Home Pay	$_____	$_____
2. Present Credit Obligations	$_____	$_____
3. Your Debt Ratio	_____%	_____%

3. Your Debt Ratio
   Divide your credit
   obligations (line 2) by your
   take home pay (line 3)
   *Note—It should not exceed 20%

Figure 8-2 Calculating Your Personal Debt Ratio

CHAPTER 9

TEACHING YOUR CHILDREN MONEY MANAGEMENT

Today's black children are our future leaders. Black parents can begin to prepare their children for this role by teaching them about the world of business and high finance.

Teaching children the value and power of money at an early age will increase their interest in obtaining financial assets and give them the critical edge to survive in this competitive global economy. It will also teach them to become independent, successful and economically prosperous at a much earlier age than past generations.

You are your children's best teacher. They learn from examples. By taking time with your children in this area right now, you will raise children who have a financial awareness and will manage money instead of being managed by it.

Many parents in middle class black families have a tendency to shower their children with expensive toys and clothes having a certain status symbol. Parents should not try to compensate for what they missed while growing up. Such behavior can have two detrimental effects on the children. 1) It prevents your children from developing the attitude of self-sufficiency. And 2) it brings about ungrateful children who have the instant gratification syndrome. When these children leave home it is very difficult for them to continue with the same life-style that their parents have provided. As a result many are not willing to start out at the bottom of the career ladder and work their way up or work for minimum wage. Instead they resort to illegal means of obtaining money —the underground economy—to obtain instant wealth.

Begin discussing the family finances with your children. When paying monthly bills, have children participate. Many times children don't understand that you must pay for water, heat and a place to live. They assume it is free. Expose them to all aspects of your budgeting system.

When a child asks for something, don't just say "no you can't have it because I said so." Explain to them it doesn't fit into the budget this month and they will need to save their money and buy it for themselves. The child then understands that money doesn't just magically appear and that they cannot always have what they want. Reasoning with children this way helps to relieve the blame and pressure the child may impose on the parent.

Allowances—Savings

Many parents are unsure as to whether or not a child should receive an allowance and at what age it should start. Yes, giving children a weekly allowance gives them spending money and it also makes them feel like part of the family. There really isn't any best age to start, but experts feel between the ages of 3 and 6. By that time most children understand numbers.

Have your child start a savings account and a piggy bank as soon as they learn how to count. There are still banks and savings and loans that allow for small deposits without a fee. Shop around. A great bank especially for children is the *First Children's Bank* located in one of the world's largest toy stores, FAO Schwarz in New York City. The bank is for children under the age of 18 or 21, if they own a college certificate of deposit. They offer checking, savings and CDs—certificates of deposits. The First Children's Bank offers 2 children's publications—a coloring book called *Saving Money Is Smart*, and a comic book titled *The Buck Starts Here*. If you do not live in the New York area they also offer banking by mail. You can request the publications by writing or calling The First Children's Bank,

111 E. 57 St., New York, NY 10022; (212) 644-0670.

The Illinois State Treasurer's office offers a bank-at-school program that has been successful in the inner city schools of Chicago. In the program, African-American elementary school children serve as banking officers and actually run the bank, thereby learning money management skills through first-hand experience. The children are encouraged to improve their spending habits and to start a savings program with just $10.

This and similar programs are excellent ways to teach African-American students to lay down a basic foundation for successful money management habits which they will carry into their adult lives. Parents everywhere need to insist that their children's schools develop such a program. You can start by contacting the Illinois State Treasurer's office for more information on its program. It's listed in the resources section at the back of this book.

Explain to your children that part of their allowance must be placed in a savings account for long term to pay for college or a car. Encourage them to set long term goals as you yourself do. If your child spends all of her allowance before the next due date don't give in and give more money. This will hinder your child in learning to manage money and credit later in life. If you have extra jobs around the house, pay your child to do them. It's an excellent way for them to earn extra money and to learn skills that will help them become financially independent. Studies have shown that children who earn their own spending money have a much higher self-esteem and take these skills to become financially independent in their adult life.

Another area where children can learn about money management is in gift giving. Toys today are expensive and it is not unusual to spend over $100 for 1 toy that will more than likely end up in the closet after a few weeks when the excitment has worn off. Instead of buying nothing but toys for birthday and Christmas presents buy shares of stock in the toy company or any company that the child can relate to. You can assist them with following the stock in the newspaper. You can also help them with reading the company's annual report. If there is a stockholder's meeting in your area you and your child should attend. This is another way of exposing them to all facets of the business world.

You can explain to your children that they own a part of the company and as the company makes money they make money. The $100 that they would have spent on the new video game, and would have eventually grown tired of, could possibly grow to $500. By explaining to children how money works and grows you will find many of them will forgo purchasing so many toys and will insist on obtaining money to save and invest for future use. This type of behavior leads to financial empowerment in adult life.

It is also time that you limit the amount of time and what programs your children watch on television. Encourage them to watch business programs such as CNBC lo-

cated on cable and Wall Street Week. Discuss daily what happened on Wall Street and what is in the business section of the local paper. Fill your home with business magazines and books. If there is any news regarding your company share it with them. If you want your children to develop an appetite for business you must provide the material to stimulate them. Keeping informed about the business climate is a key element of success.

When successful business owners and corporate executives were asked what led them to become successful, many stated that it was common that business and financial issues were discussed around the dinner table. By the time they were in school they knew a great deal about money and business. They understood the importance of managing money. If we want our children to become successful business owners and executives then we must do the same. Begin today by turning off the television set at dinner time and discussing business and world events. Make learning a family affair.

If you currently do not have an investment portfolio to share with your children, develop an imaginary stock and bond portfolio. Make each person in the family responsible for studying and researching a stock that they like. Teach them to read the stock pages and notice the enthusiasm they will have once they start making money.

There is now a no-load mutual fund whose aim is to teach children how to invest. Called the Young Investor Fund, it is sponsored by Stein Roe & Farnham. The fund invests money heavily in companies that children can identify with such as McDonald's, Toys-Я-Us, Coca-Cola, and Microsoft. The minimum to start the account is $500 if you participate in their monthly purchasing plan, otherwise it's $1,000.

The object of the fund is to make investing fun. Once the kids invest they receive a welcome kit that includes a young investor's certificate, a large wall poster for tracking their investments, and a ''You and Your Money'' activity book that includes money games and takes a light approach to teaching investment concepts.

Teach your children to save at least 10% of their allowance or money earned from odd jobs. If they develop the 10% savings habit while they are young, it will more than likely continue in their adult life. Set up a savings notebook for your children, so they can keep track of their money. Introduce them to your banker, tax accountant, stockbroker, financial planner and insurance agent. Ask for a tour of the office and a brief discussion with your child explaining the importance of their particular area in financial management.

When your child is in junior high school begin discussing college cost. They should be made responsible for paying part of their college tuition. A good incentive program to help your child save money is a **matching program**, which is a similar program offered to employees in corporations. For every dollar that they save you will match with 25 or 50 cents, and you will pay it at the end of every month. The matching program should be stated in writing and agreed upon by both you and your child.

Entrepreneurship

Encourage your child to start their own business. The days of the lemonade stand may be over but there are plenty of hobbies or products that your child can become involved with. The new decade is dictating to Black Americans the necessity of having one's own business. Teaching children today the benefits of having their own business will prepare them to become self-reliant and independent. It will teach them to solve their own problems and make their own way. If they have a business to focus on after school hours it will help eliminate children standing on the street corner.

Help your children start an **Own Your Own Business Club**. Contact the school or Parent Teachers Association in your neighborhood and suggest a program be started. Have Black business owners in the community talk about their experiences and what they did to get started. The business owners will serve as role models and teach your children how to start a business.

If we want to see our children succeed in this competitive society, we should follow the advice of the late Reginald Lewis, who was the first African-American entrepreneur to build a billion dollar empire. He was an advocate of teaching children about business. He frequently talked to young children and encouraged them to become successful by setting goals and having the determination to succeed regardless of the limits society places on them. He told African-Americans students not to allow racism to pull them down and urged girls to get busy working toward their goals rather than watching television and playing house.

Careers in Finance

If your child is not interested in starting her own business then expose her to careers in finance and business. There are careers in the banking and securities industries that you may not be aware of. Read the February issue of Black Enterprise magazine, which publishes an annual career and opportunities guide that lists several careers in the business and financial area.

For additional information on educational programs to assist you in teaching your children about finances contact the programs that are listed in the appendix.

■ **NOTES**

_____

_____

_____

_____

_____

_____

_____

_____

_____

_____

_____

PART 2

WINNING TAX AND SAVINGS STRATEGIES

CHAPTER 10

INSURANCE—PROTECTING YOUR ASSETS

Insurance is the least exciting yet most misunderstood part of your financial plan, but it is the most important. It protects what you have and assures that unexpected events such as illness, death or serious property damage do not undermine what you have planned for the future.

Traditionally life insurance was purchased for men only, since they were considered the breadwinners of the family. Times have changed and many women should now be covered, particularly in the Black community where there are many single mothers with sole support of their children.

Life insurance is primarily for financial protection of your dependents in the event you die young. It will replace the income that stops and provide money for the education and basic living needs of your young children. So if you are not presently financially well-off, life insurance is a must for women with family responsibilities. For a single woman with no dependents, life insurance isn't always a necessity. It depends on the amount of your assets and liabilities. If you are employed, most likely you have coverage through your employer and it may be enough to cover your final expenses.

If you are a married working mother with young children, at today's standard of living, your income is a necessary part of the family income. So your insurance should cover your income as well.

Single mothers who work and provide the sole support of their children should without a doubt have life insurance coverage until the children are no longer dependent on them.

Because insurance is so misunderstood and confusing, many women are either over insured (paying too much in premiums) or under insured (not buying enough).

To better understand and take more control of your life insurance cost, here are a few terms you should understand before talking to an agent:

- **Death Benefit (face value)**—the amount of money that is paid to the beneficiary if the insured person dies.
- **Premium**—the amount you pay to the in-

surance company for coverage. It can be paid monthly, quarterly, or annually.

- **Policy Term**—the period of time you are covered by life insurance. It can range from one year to your lifetime.
- **Surrender Charge**—a fee charged by the insurance company if you cancel your policy. It can run into several thousand dollars. So before you sign on the dotted line, question whether or not your policy has a surrender charge.

Types of Life Insurance

The two basic types of life insurance are *Term* and *Whole-Life*. Within these 2 categories there are various types of policies.

Term Insurance

Term insurance, life insurance for a specific period of time with no frills or a savings plan, is the least expensive life insurance you can buy. The coverage provides protection only, and pays when the insured person dies.

It is most practical for women with young children and young couples, providing the greatest amount of protection for the least amount of money.

There are 3 types of term insurance:

Annual Renewable Term

This is insurance with a term of 1 year renewable yearly. The premium begins at a low rate, and increases each year, the younger you are the lower the beginning rates. This is the least expensive of the 3 types of term insurance and the most recommended. It is guaranteed renewable annually as long as you continue to pay your premium.

Decreasing Term

Decreasing term is mainly used as mortgage insurance to pay off your home mortgage. Your annual premium stays the same, but the amount of your insurance declines over time. This coverage is far too expensive for the amount of coverage that you receive.

Level Term

This is the most disadvantageous of the 3 because you are prepaying the premiums for the beginning years. The premium and the protection stays the same throughout the designated policy period. Essentially you are allowing the insurance company the use of your money, preventing you from obtaining a higher return elsewhere. If you cancel your policy you lose all of the upfront premium payments. This is not a policy for an individual trying to reach financial independence.

Whole-Life Insurance

Whole-life insurance is insurance that provides protection as well as a savings plan. The premiums are higher than term insurance because of the savings feature. The amount of the premium is determined by your age at the time you buy the policy and stays the same as long as the policy is in effect.

In the beginning a small percentage of your premium is credited to your savings account which accumulates a cash surrender value. If you cancel the policy this savings accumulation remains yours. If you wish to borrow against the cash surrender value you may do so by paying an interest rate stated in the contract, keeping the policy in force and continuing to pay the premiums. If you die, the insurance company will deduct the amount of the loan from the amount it pays the beneficiary.

The problem with whole-life insurance is that it is sold as a tax-deferred savings plan. But in reality your savings could be earning a much higher interest in your own investment portfolio. Also, the beneficiaries of the policy do not receive the accumulated cash value in addition to the face value. They receive only the face value. For example, you have a policy with a face value of $100,000 with an accumulated cash value of $10,000. If you were to die your beneficiary would receive the $100,000 face value, not $110,000; which includes the accumulated cash value. So if you can't motivate yourself to save money, then whole insurance may be for you. Otherwise stick to term insurance to receive more protection for less money.

Universal Life

A new type of insurance on the market is universal life insurance. It is similar to whole-life in that a portion of the premium pays for insurance while the other portion goes into a savings fund. It differs in offering more flexibility than whole-life, since interest earned on the savings plan can be either at a fixed rate or placed into mutual funds. Because the fees and commission charges on this type of insurance can be expensive, it is more advantageous to purchase term insurance and have your own investment plan.

How Much Life Insurance Do You Need?

If you fall into the category of needing life insurance, the next question is how much do you need? Using your monthly income requirement figure and assuming you could invest the insurance proceeds at a fixed rate, **Worksheet 10-1** shows you a quick and easy formula to calculate your insurance coverage needs. If you have children and want a more accurate amount, **Worksheet 10-2** will include your social security income, savings and college cost of children.

Married Women and Life Insurance

Many men do not believe in buying life insurance. If your spouse falls into this category, you should have a policy on his life and pay for it yourself. Many women have been left financially strapped after the death of their spouse because the husband did not believe in insurance.

Insurance Coverage (Quick Simple Formula)

Monthly Income Requirement	$3,500
Months Per Year	× 12
Annual Income Requirement	$42,000
Interest Rate 9%	Divided by 9%
Insurance Coverage Needed	$466,667

10-1 Insurance Coverage (Quick Simple Formula)

How Insurance Proceeds Are Paid

When an insured person dies there are several ways the beneficiary can receive the insurance proceeds. Here are the options:

• **Lump Sum**—You receive the full payment for the amount of the proceeds immediately (minus any amount that has been borrowed from the insurance policy). This is the best option because you can invest the proceeds to meet your individual needs, and receive a much higher return than by letting the insurance company invest the money for you.

• **Fixed Installments**—At a specific time you receive a fixed amount of money until you are completely paid out. The insurance company continues to pay interest on the unpaid balance.

• **Interest Only**—Here the insurance company pays you interest only and continues to hold the principle. Before you select this option, be sure to compare the interest rates that the insurance company is offering with interest rates you could receive from your own investment program.

Other Types of Insurance

Disability Insurance

One of the most valuable assets you have is your ability to work and earn an income. The chance of your becoming disabled by an accident far outweighs your chance of death. With a decrease in income and most

Figuring out How Much Life Insurance

The purpose of life insurance is to guarantee your family a comfortable life if you die young. Consequently you should err on the high side when calculating your coverage. That does not mean sacrificing all present niceties for the possibility of turning your relatives into Rockefellers. It does mean carrying enough protection to preserve your family's current standard of living. You can arrive at a suitable amount of coverage by using this worksheet. If both spouses have paying jobs, make a copy of the worksheet and do the figures for each breadwinner.

This exercise aims to nail down how much insurance you need while your children are growing up. It does not include the much larger sums required to finance a surviving spouse's later life or retirement. The presumption these days is that he or she could take care of that. But families with lifelong dependents—a handicapped child, for example—should ask a financial planner for help in their calculations.

Most of the lines on the worksheet explain themselves. Here's some coaching for those that don't:

Line 1. In two-paycheck households, start by lumping together both after-tax incomes. Payroll deductions for the retirement funds and health insurance count as take-home pay; life insurance deductions do not.

Line 2. People usually spend a third of their income on themselves. You may want to figure more or less than that.

Line 6. In totaling your present assets, don't forget Individual Retirement Accounts, company savings plans and survivor's benefits from your pension fund.

Lines 7 and 8. Consider here whether your spouse, if she or he is now working, would wish to stay home with the children for a year or two if you die. Then subtract that year or two from the number on line 4. If your spouse would choose not to work for several years, don't count on any take-home pay. Enter 0 on line 7.

Line 10. Social security survivor benefits can become a major source of income. Table A,

(continued)

1. Current total family take-home pay $_____
2. One-third of your own take-home pay $_____
3. Annual family expenses without you (line 1 minus line 2) $_____
4. Number of years until your youngest child finishes high school $_____
5. Total family expenses (line 3 times line 4) $_____
6. Savings and investments $_____
7. Spouse's annual take-home pay $_____
8. Number of years of that income $_____
9. Total spouse contribution (line 7 times line 8) $_____
10. Total social security benefits $_____
11. Total assets and income (add lines 6, 9 and 10) $_____
12. Total income deficit $_____
13. Average annual income deficit (line 5 minus line 11) $_____
14. Lump sum that, if invested, would provide the amount on line 13 for the number of years on line 4 (factor from Table B times $1,000) $_____
15. College costs per child $_____
16. Number of college-bound children   ×_____
17. Total college costs $_____
18. Funeral and estate costs $_____
19. Lump sum for a mortgage or emergency fund (optional) $_____
20. Total lump sum needed at death (add lines 14, 17, 18 and 19) $_____
21. Present insurance needed $_____
22. Total insurance needed (line 20 minus line 2) (if negative, you have more than you need) $_____

Worksheet 10-2 Figuring out How Much Life Insurance
Reprinted with permission. Copyright 1987. Money Magazine.

at right, indicates the annual amounts currently paid to a non-working spouse and children and the maximum available per family. Benefits decline swiftly for a working spouse earning more than $6,000 a year. Children continue collecting until they graduate from high school or turn 19, whichever comes first. A spouse's benefits expire after the youngest child reaches 16. Estimate your total benefits by counting the years of maximum and lesser benefits at your income level in the table. Multiply the benefits by the number of years you would like to collect them and add the results. (For further help, call your local Social Security office or write to the Social Security Administration, Office of Public Inquiries, Baltimore, MD 21235.)

Line 14. The average annual income deficit resulting from your death (line 13) overstates what your family would need unless you adjust the amount for investment income. Much of the lump sum you are calculating could earn interest or dividends for several years before the whole amount is spent. The number shown in table B, at left, most nearly corresponding to your annual deficit and the years your family would need income (line 4) is a factor that, when multiplied by $1,000, approximates the lump sum needed. It is based on the conservative assumption that after taxes and inflation the fund would earn 2% return.

Line 15. Enter an amount here if you want your insurance to finance the college education of your child or children. Four years at a private college, including room and board, now costs an average of $40,100, and public colleges average $22,416. For children at least 5 years away from college, those amounts should be adjusted now for inflation. Assuming 5% annual increases, raise them to $52,000 and $28,6000 —and in 5 years review them against actual costs.

Line 18. Funeral and estate costs including the settlement of debts, generally amount to 1 year's take home pay.

Line 19. If you wish, you can provide money that your family could use to pay off the mortgage or keep for emergencies.

Line 21. Take into account any coverage you already have from your employer as well as your own policies.

FIGURING OUT HOW MUCH LIFE INSURANCE

Table A: Social security benefits. Here are estimates of annual survivor payments for your spouse and children.

Worker's Present Age		Workers 1989 Income		Over
		$20,000	$30,000	$40,000
25	Benefit per survivor	$6,312	$7,764	$9,060
	Maximum family benefit	14,940	18,132	21,132
35	Benefit per survivor	6,228	7,716	8,724
	Maximum family benefit	14,795	18,000	20,352
45	Benefit per survivor	6,216	7,488	7,944
	Maximum family benefit	14,772	17,484	18,528
55	Benefit per survivor	6,216	7,224	7,572
	Maximum family benefit	14,760	16,872	17,544
65	Benefit per survivor	5,868	6,804	7,092
	Maximum family benefit	13,908	15,888	16,560

Source: Social Security Administration

Table B: Lump-sum factors. Here are the amounts needed to replace income (multiply by $1,000)

Dollar Amount (from line 13)	Number of Years (from Line 4)								
	5	7	9	11	13	15	16	17	18
$5,000	24	33	41	49	57	65	72	79	85
10,000	48	65	82	98	114	129	143	157	170
15,000	71	98	123	147	170	193	214	235	255
20,000	95	130	164	196	227	257	286	313	340
25,000	118	163	205	245	284	321	357	391	425
30,000	142	195	245	294	340	385	428	469	510
35,000	166	227	286	343	397	449	500	548	594
40,000	189	260	327	391	454	513	571	626	679
45,000	213	292	368	440	510	578	642	704	764
50,000	236	325	408	489	567	642	713	782	849
55,000	260	357	449	538	624	706	785	860	934
60,000	283	390	490	587	680	770	856	938	1,019
65,000	307	422	531	636	737	834	927	1,016	1,104
70,000	331	454	571	685	794	898	999	1,095	1,188
75,000	354	487	612	734	850	962	1,070	1,173	1,273

Worksheet 10-2 (Continued)

likely an increase in medical bills, poor financial preparedness could create chaos in your life. To avoid such a disaster, disability insurance is available to take care of your income if you are unable to work.

Social security offers a limited disability coverage with a restrictive definition of disability; in that your case might not meet their guidelines to make you eligible. If you are eligible, you must wait 6 months before you receive the money.

Many employers and trade associations offer disability insurance for their employees as part of a benefit package. Most of these companies offer one of two disability plans. The first pays benefits for a short period usually up to 1 year. The second is the long term plan intended for more serious disabilities. The latter generally provides a certain percentage of your earnings, and payments can last 5 to 10 years or until you reach the age of 65. Like social security, many plans will not pay for at least 6 months after you have become disabled. Check with your employer to see which plan covers you. If you are not covered, you should consider an individual policy. The annual premiums tend to be expensive and are based on your age, health, and income. Check with various insurance companies and compare coverages and annual premiums.

Homeowner Insurance

Homeowner's insurance offers 2 types of protection: 1) covers your home and personal property and, 2) covers your liability for injury to others.

With homeowners insurance you want to be sure you have adequate coverage to replace your home and the contents of your home in the event of complete loss due to perils such as fires, vandalism, or other damaging events. You should consider 2 disasters not automatically covered: flood and earthquake coverage, if you live in an area where these are common. Many offer earthquake coverage. Coverage for flood is offered through a federal government program. For additional information contact the insurer.

If you are renting an apartment or condominium you also need coverage. You should have a plan that covers your personal property as well as liability for injury to others. If someone is injured in your apartment they can sue you as well as the landlord.

Due to the recent increase of lawsuits brought upon ordinary everyday people, it isn't uncommon for someone to want to sue you. This is why you need the liability protection, particularly if you are an individual with a substantial net worth and live a life that conveys the atmosphere of wealth. Doctors, attorneys, high paid entertainers, and politicians are prime targets for lawsuits.

The needed amount of liability insurance varies according to your net worth. The minimum anyone should have is $25,000 with an average of $300,000. If your net worth is above this, then consider coverage as high as $1 million.

Automobile Insurance

If you have a car, automobile insurance is no longer optional but required by law in most states. Automobile insurance is very similar to homeowner's insurance in that it covers your property (the car) and liability for bodily injury or damage to another person's property.

If you have an accident and you are at fault your insurance plan will cover the damage. It also will cover events such as theft and vandalism. You are paid either the cost of the repairs or the actual cash value, whichever is less. The actual cash value is the depreciated value of the auto before the damage, not the replacement value. Most of the time the actual cash value is a far cry from the replacement value. If you have an older car check with your agent regarding the collision and comprehensive coverage. Collision covers damage to your car caused by a collision with another auto or object. It doesn't matter whether the object is moving or not. Your collision coverage carries a deductible, which is the amount you must pay before the insurance company kicks in its share. The higher the deductible, the lower your premium. The normal deductible is $100 to $300. Comprehensive covers damages made by entities other than automobiles such as fire and theft.

Your liability coverage is the most important because it covers bodily injury, death to others, property damage, medical payments, and uninsured or under insured motorists. The uninsured or under insured

coverage is important. In spite of state laws requiring all owners of motor vehicles to carry insurance, many do not. This coverage projects you for medical injuries and loss of income; so choose the highest amount possible.

Automobile insurance is a necessity and cost varies city to city. Shop around and compare rates. If you live in a large city your rates are likely to be 2 to 4 times higher than a small city where traffic is less heavy and accidents are less likely to occur. Make sure you have enough liability coverage and review and update your policy yearly.

Health Insurance

A large percentage of us are covered by health insurance through our employer. Lately, health and medical costs have skyrocketed in that many companies are now requiring you to pay a larger percentage of the cost.

With the increase of layoffs and merging of companies, many black women are finding themselves not only without a job but also without health insurance. For a single mother with young children, a major illness could have a detrimental effect on your finances. It is imperative that you understand your present health coverage and various types of other coverage. Health insurance is to protect you from high hospital bills, doctor fees and drugs.

The best type of health insurance is one that provides basic protection and major medical coverage for long-term illnesses.

The basic protection coverage pays a percentage of your doctor and hospital bill and other medical expenses up to a specified amount. The coverage is also limited to a certain number of days during each illness. If your illness lasts longer than the basic coverage, then the major medical coverage begins and covers the large expenses from long-term hospitalization, surgery, private duty nursing, doctor bills, therapy, and rehabilitation. Most major medical coverage requires you to pay an annual deductible before the benefits begin. Once that is paid, the policy pays 80 to 85% of the cost, and you pay the balance. Major medical policies will cover you, your spouse and children under the age of 19, if the child is in school—up to 23 years old.

You should also be aware of a law passed in 1986. It states that if you lose your job with a company that has more than 20 employees offering group health insurance and you were not dismissed because of disorderly conduct, the former employer is required to supply health insurance for a year and a half or until you receive a job offering health insurance, whichever comes first. Also, if you get divorced or your spouse dies, the spouse's employer must provide you with the right to continue the health insurance policy at a cost to you for up to 3 years.

Medicare

If you are 65 years or older and eligible for social security you are entitled to Medicare. If you are under 65 and disabled you are also eligible.

Medicare provides free of charge, hospital bills and care in a nursing home. It pays 80% of normal medical costs for doctor fees, outpatient services and certain medical supplies and services. It will not pay for dentistry, private nursing, or eyeglasses. Senior citizens will need supplemental health insurance to pay these medical expenses. Without it, a major illness can completely wipe out your retirement nest egg.

HMO—Health Maintenance Organization

An alternative to traditional health insurance is the HMO—which is very popular in many states, particularly in California. Many employers are now offering HMO's as a part of the employee benefit package.

In an HMO there is no deductible and you pay a flat fee each year plus a $3 to $5 per office visit charge. You are entitled to medical care 24 hours a day, seven days a week at particular hospitals and clinics owned by the HMO. The greatest disadvantage is that you cannot choose a doctor outside of the HMO plan. And many do not provide coverage for dental care and eye care. Before signing with an HMO plan, call the state agency that regulates the HMO in your area and talk with some of the existing members.

Summary

Insurance plays an important part in your total financial plan. You should have all of the insurance coverage in this chapter before you begin your investment portfolio. Shop around and be cautious of salespeople who try to sell you unneeded coverage. Compare companies, coverage and rates. Annually review your insurance program.

■ NOTES

_____

_____

_____

_____

_____

_____

_____

_____

_____

_____

_____

_____

_____

_____

_____

_____

CHAPTER 11

TAX PLANNING STRATEGIES

Keeping More of What You Make

During your lifetime you will pay the federal government thousands of your hard earned dollars. That is if you don't have a tax planning strategy. It isn't how much income you make but how much of your income you actually get to keep for spending and investing. Year-round tax planning is an essential step to becoming financially independent. New tax laws are passed every year and it is essential to understand their effects and the strategies you can implement to reduce your taxes. In order to keep abreast of the new tax laws it is advisable to meet annually with your tax advisor.

The latest major tax overhaul signed into law is the Revenue Reconciliation Act (RRA). The focus of the act is to close many of the tax loopholes and increase rates to wealthy taxpayers. Under this new legislation the following changes have been made:

- A new 36% marginal rate is imposed on taxable income over $143,600 for married couples filing joint returns; $130,800 for heads of households; $117,950 for single people; and $128,250 for married couples

filing separately. The RRA further imposed a 10% surtax on individuals with taxable income in excess of $250,000, increasing the 36% marginal rate to 39.6%. The tax brackets are outlined in **Figure 11-1**.

- The tax code now phases out the deductions for personal exemptions when your adjusted gross income exceeds $111,800 for single filers; $167,700 for joint returns; $139,750 for heads of households; and $83,850 for married couples who file separate returns. The exemption amount will be phased out by 2% for each $2,500 (or any portion thereof) of adjusted gross income that exceeds the above amounts.

- The tax law also reduces the benefit of itemized deductions for certain high-income taxpayers. Your itemized deductions, other than those for medical, casualty and theft losses, and investment interest, will be reduced by an amount equal to 3% of both single and married taxpayers with adjusted gross incomes in excess of $111,800 (this amount will be adjusted annually for inflation). However, there are a couple of restrictions. Your itemized deducations can't be reduced by more than 80%. And the phaseout does not affect the medical, casualty and theft, or investment interest deductions.

- Taxpayers will now pay higher social security taxes and the Medicare tax will be paid through withholding from your wages. If you're self-employed, you'll be hit the hardest because you will have to pay both the employer and employee rate on a combined basis.

The following tax-reducing breaks are still in effect, be sure to take advantage of them:

- Deduction of mortgage interest on your first and second home.
- Deduction of state and local income, real estate, and property tax
- Keogh deduction for self-employed individuals
- Child care tax credit
- Deduction of casualty and theft losses
- Deduction of alimony support
- The tax-deferred earnings on IRAs, Keoghs, life insurance and annuities.

Tax-Saving Investments and Strategies

Since Black women earn on average, 54% less than men, it is even more important that you take all possible legal tax deductions and devise tax-saving strategies in order to keep most of what you make.

There are basically 2 ways to reduce your

tax bill, 1) You can defer the taxes and pay them in the future, preferably when your income is lower, or 2) you can avoid paying taxes completely, which of course is the better of the two. But, unfortunately, because of the new tax laws, there are few ways to actually avoid taxes altogether.

Before starting your tax-reducing plan, you should know your adjusted gross income and taxable income. The easiest way is to refer to your latest 1040 (long form) line 31 or 1040EZ (short form) line 3. If that isn't available, list all your income, earned, investment, and passive on a sheet of paper and on another sheet list all your allowable deductions (this information is available from the IRS tax form) and compute the difference. Then refer to **Figure 11-1**, to find your tax bracket.

The next step is to lower your income even more and pay even less in taxes through the following tax-reducing investments and strategies:

Timing of Your Income

Deferring the time you receive your income can defer the payment of income taxes. There are several ways that this can be accomplished:

- If your company regularly gives out bonuses, negotiate with your employer to pay you in the following year.
- If you're a business owner, you can accelerate your payment of business expenses or delay the mailing of bills or

invoices so that you forestall the collection of income.

- If you're getting ready to retire, consider delaying the retirement benefit payout to a later date when your income is lower.
- Consider investments such as treasury bills, U.S. Government Series EE Savings Bonds, and certificates of deposit. Make sure you time the investment to mature into the following year. That way, you won't receive the interest income until then.

Charitable Contributions

Contributions to African-American charitable organizations is a way to be socially responsible and at the same time save on income taxes. Make sure to obtain a receipt from the charity stating the amount of your donation. The tax law states that any contribution over $250 must be substantiated in writing by the charity. You must have the receipt in your possession at the time you file your tax return. Previously, a cancelled check was enough to satisfy the IRS, but that is no longer the case.

Owning Your Own Home

This is one of the last remaining available tax shelters. The mortgage interest and property taxes are still fully deductible. And you can defer taxes on the capital gain on the sale of your home as long as you buy another home costing as much or more than

the one you sold within a 2 year time frame.

Sale of Your Home

If you're at least 55 years of age, and you sell your principal residence, you may receive a substantial income tax benefit from the Internal Revenue Service—a once-in-a-lifetime choice to exclude up to $125,000 of gain from the sale. In order to qualify for the deduction, you must have owned and occupied the house for 3 of the 5 years preceding the sale. If the property is held jointly with your spouse, only one of you must meet the age requirement to qualify for the deduction.

If you're not yet 55 years of age you can still defer taxes on the sale of your personal residence by reinvesting the money in a house of equal or greater cost. The benefit is available as long as you purchase your new home within 2 years after the sale of the old one.

Capital Gains Tax

There is a 28% ceiling on the income tax you pay on the net capital gains you receive from the sale of your long-term investments. These would include stocks, mutual funds, bonds, and real estate (the definition of long term is when you hold an investment longer than 1 year and 1 day). If you receive a gain on any investments held for less than this time they are taxed at your highest marginal tax rate.

Review Your Property Tax Appraisal

With the recent decline in the value of real estate you may be paying too much in property taxes. In most areas, property assessments increase each year whether or not your home value rises. You may be able to dispute your appraisal and lower your property tax bill's thereby saving yourself money by contacting the county assessor's office in your city.

Alternative Minimum Tax

The alternative minimum tax is one part of the tax code that is confusing to many people. It was instituted by the Internal Revenue Service in an attempt to close the tax loopholes that wealthy taxpayers were using to pay almost no income taxes at all. If you fall in the 36% or 39.6% tax rate you may be liable to alternative minimum taxes. I recommend you consult with your certified public accountant (CPA) or tax advisor to find out more about this possibility.

Individual Retirement Account (IRA)

Depending on your level of income, and if you or your spouse are covered by a company retirement program, your individual retirement contribution (IRA) deduction may be limited or completely eliminated. In spite of this, the IRA is still a great way to shelter income. The taxes on the earnings of the IRA are deferred until the money is actually withdrawn (more on IRAs in chapter 14).

Keogh Retirement Plan for Self-Employed Women

If you are a self-employed woman, regardless of whether it is full time or part time from moonlighting, you can have a tax shelter called a Keogh plan. A Keogh plan allows you to shelter up to 25% of your net (after tax) self-employment income or a maximum of $30,000 whichever is less (more on Keoghs in Chapter 14).

Employer Retirement Program

If you work in a company that offers a 401(k) salary reduction savings plan, do not pass it up. It is a great way to save money and save on taxes as well. As an incentive to invest in the company, many of the plans offer a match of all or part of your contribution. The money is taken out of your paycheck before taxes are taken out, helping to lower your taxable income. The earnings are also tax deferred until you withdraw the money. Contribute as much as you can into your 401(k) up to a maximum of $9,240 a year (this amount adjusts annually for inflation). The only catch is that if you withdraw the money before you are 59½ years old, not only do you pay the taxes on the amount but the government imposes a 10% penalty fee. (more on employer retirement programs in chapter 14).

Retirement Rollovers

Many corporations are reducing their workforces by offering employees early retirement packages. If you are considering such a package, you need to understand the tax ramifications.

A distribution received prior to the age of 59½ from a qualified retirement plan such as a 401(k), 403(b), or IRA is taxed as ordinary income on receipt and is subject to a 10% excise tax penalty. This penalty can be avoided by depositing the distribution in a rollover IRA within 60 days of receiving the money.

Distributions from these plans are also subject to a withholding tax in the amount of 20% of the eligible rollover amount. This money is to be withheld by the plan trustee (employer) unless the employee (that's you) instructs the trustee to transfer it directly to another qualified retirement plan or IRA.

Review Your Withholding

Check with your tax advisor to determine if you are claiming enough withholdings. This amount along with your estimated payments should be high enough to avoid underpayment penalities but low enough to avoid loaning your money to Uncle Sam for a year without interest. Contrary to what most people think, getting a large tax refund is not smart money management. You have allowed the IRS to use your money without paying you interest.

Income Tax Credits

Tax credits will reduce your regular income tax liability dollar for dollar. The major tax credit to consider is the:

Dependent and Child Care Credit
You can claim a tax credit of 20%–30% (based on the amount of your income) for eligible expenses paid for the care of qualified individuals such as children or a spouse incapable of self-care. You may even claim day care and babysitting expenses as long as all the other requirements are met. If you are married, the expenses are limited to the earned income of the spouse with the lower income.

If you claim the dependent care tax credit, you are required to include the name, address, federal identification number of the organization, and the social security number of the person providing the care.

Tax-Free Money Market Funds

These funds allow you to earn tax-free interest on your money. It is a mutual fund that invests in short-term municipal bonds. The interest is free from federal taxes and sometimes free of state and local taxes. You can withdraw money from a tax free money market fund at any time, which is why it is a good place to put your money for the short term. In order to benefit from tax-free income you should be in the top tax bracket, 28%–39.6%.

Municipal Bonds

These bonds are issued by states, cities, and counties and the interest is federally tax free. If it is a bond issued by the state in which you live it is also state tax free. Municipal bonds are not advantageous for everyone. Chapter 18 will discuss municipal bonds in more depth.

Annuities/Single Premium Whole-life Insurance

Annuities are tax-deferred investments that are issued and backed by life insurance companies. The earnings from annuities are tax-deferred until the money is withdrawn. For example, if you invest $10,000 in an annuity earning 9% at the end of the year, your account will equal $10,900. Until you withdraw from your account, taxes are not due and the money compounds tax sheltered.

Two types of annuities are *fixed* and *variable*. A fixed annuity is sometimes called a single premium deferred annuity (SPDA). Single premium deferered annuities offer a guaranteed rate of return, guaranteed principal, tax-deferred interest and avoid probate. Probate means in case of the death of the annuitant (the person who owns the annuity contract) the beneficiary immediately receives the death benefit and avoids going through the court. Probate will be discussed further in chapter 23.

There is typically a minimum of $5,000 to invest in a single premium deferred annuity, and the guaranteed rate of return is for a specific period of time, usually 1 or 5 years. After that, the interest rate changes according to the current market rate. Many single premium deferred annuities have bail-out clauses which allow you to withdraw your money without a fee if the interest rate drops 1 or 2 percentage points below your initial guaranteed rate. Example: You invest in a 1 year annuity at 8% which has a bail-out rate of 7%. At the end of 1 year, if the new rate is below 7% you have the right to withdraw your money without a fee.

A variable annuity is for someone who is interested in more growth and variety. These are also issued and backed by life insurance companies. Many variable annuities allow you to invest as little as $1,500.

The major difference between a fixed and variable annuity is that the variable annuity offers a fixed rate of return as well as investments in stocks, bonds, and money market mutual funds. You are allowed to choose the investment and can switch among the portfolios to match your changing financial objectives. The investment funds are managed by professional money managers and the rate of growth of the annuity is dependent upon their investment results. Similar to the fixed annuity, the variable annuity earnings are also tax-deferred until the money is withdrawn.

Most annuities charge either a front or back-end sales commission which can range from 3 to 8% of the amount you invest. In addition there is an annual administrative fee of 1.5%. Most annuities allow you to withdraw up to 10% of the amount you invest

Tax Rates 1995

Married Filing Joint Return

Taxable Income	Not Over	Your Tax Is:	Of the Amount Over:
$0	$ 38,000	15%,	$0
38,000	91,850	$ 5,700.00 + 28%	38,000
91,850	140,000	20,778.00 + 31%	91,850
140,000	250,000	35,704.50 + 36%	140,000
250,000	over	75,304.50 + 39.6%	250,000

Individual Return

Taxable Income	Not Over	Your Tax Is:	Of the Amount Over:
$0	$ 23,350	15%,	$0
23,350	56,550	$ 3,502.50 + 28%	23,350
56,550	117,950	12,798.50 + 31%	56,550
117,950	256,500	31,832.50 + 36%	117,950
256,500	over	81,710.50 + 39.6%	256,500

Head of Household Return

Taxable Income	Not Over	Your Tax Is:	Of the Amount Over:
$0	$ 31,250	15%	$0
31,250	80,750	$ 4,687.50 + 28%	31,250
80,750	130,800	18,547.50 + 31%	80,750
130,800	256,500	34,063.00 + 36%	130,800
256,500	over	79,315.00 + 39.6%	256,500

Married Filing Separate Return

Taxable Income	Not Over	Your Tax Is:	Of the Amount Over:
$0	$ 19,500	15%,	$0
19,500	47,125	$ 2,925.00 + 28%	19,500
47,125	71,800	10,660.00 + 31%	47,125
71,800	128,250	18,309.25 + 36%	71,800
128,250	over	38,631.25 + 39.6%	128,250

Figure 11-1 Tax Rates

each year without a fee. If you withdraw more, there is a 5 to 8% surrender charge during the first year which then declines for each successive year. The surrender charge disappears in 7 to 10 years. If you withdraw money from your annuity before you reach age 59½, the IRS tacks on an additional penalty of 10%. So before you invest in an annuity make sure it's for long term.

Single Premium Whole Life

Single premium whole life (SPWL) is primarily an investment vehicle that combines with a life insurance policy. Because of the life insurance policy, the earnings from SPWL are allowed to compound tax free. Unlike regular insurance, the premium of single premium whole life is paid all at one time. The minimum you can invest is $5,000 with a maximum of $500,000.

The SPWL offers safety of principal with a 100% money back guarantee. If you surrender your policy you are guaranteed to get your money minus any outstanding loans. The earnings accumulate tax free like an annuity. The interest is competitive with bank certificates of deposits. You can borrow from the accumulated interest at a very low rate of 3 to 8%, but your actual net cost of borrowing is usually zero because the interest on the loan equals your return on the amount borrowed. Death benefits from the SPWL are free of federal income taxes.

The single premium whole life is an excellent tax shelter if you have a large sum of money to invest and do not need current income. And it is also a way to accumulate money for your child's education.

Limited Partnerships

During the 1980s, limited partnerships as tax shelters were popular. They allowed you to write off more than you invested, but most of these somewhat high risk investments have been eliminated. Today, you can still shelter income through low write-off limited partnerships whose deductions are smaller. In these investments your cash distribution can be sheltered by write-offs from depreciation, mortgage interest and other management expenses.

Many of these programs are real estate partnerships, where the money is invested in apartment complexes, office buildings, warehouses, and retirement homes. There are also other limited partnerships where the money is invested in equipment leasing, cable, oil, and gas. If a limited partnership does not borrow money, it is called an all-cash limited partnership and is primarily an income-generating investment instead of a tax shelter.

When investing in limited partnerships, the safest programs are public and registered with the Securities and Exchange Commission. Most programs have a minimum of $5,000 ($2,000 for IRAs).

The drawback of partnerships is that they are illiquid (difficult to sell). They require you to leave your money in for 5 to 20 years, until all property is sold and the partnership is closed. If you want to sell before the closing date, you are apt to receive substantially less than what you paid. The income generated from limited partnerships is considered passive income and you can only write off against passive losses. Passive means you, the investor, do not actively participate in the management of the program.

Income shifting

The tax law still allows you to shift income into your child's name. The drawback is there are now added restrictions and you cannot shift as much. Previously you could put money in a trust or custodial account for your child and the earnings on the money were taxed at the child's rate, which meant little or no taxes. The law states, you can set up a custodial account for your child, but if he or she is under the age of 14, the first $600 of unearned income is exempt from taxes. The next $600 is subject to a 15% tax, and any unearned income above $1,200 will be taxed at the parents' highest marginal tax rate. Children over 14 pay regular taxes on all their unearned income.

Once money is placed in a custodial account, the money legally becomes the child's. When they reach the age of maturity, which in most states is 18 years old, the child can then do whatever they please with the money. If you want to avoid this aspect of the custodial account, there are alternatives which will be discussed in chapter 13.

Rental Property and Second Homes

Investment real estate and vacation homes are still considered good tax shelters. You can still deduct mortgage interest and property taxes you pay on your second home as long as you use it more than 14 days a year or 10% of the number of days you rent it out, whichever is more.

The amount you can write off for rental property is determined by the size of your income and whether you personally manage the property. You can deduct mortgage interest, depreciation, property taxes and other expenses for the property as long as the amount does not exceed your rental income plus any passive partnership income. If your expenses are more than your income, you can deduct up to $25,000 of the property losses against your earned and investment income as long as your adjusted gross income is less than $100,000 and you own at least 10% of the property and actively manage it.

If your adjusted gross income is $150,000 or more, you cannot deduct losses from your passive income, which is the income from rental property, and limited partnerships. So if you are considering purchasing rental property strictly for the write-off, forget it. You should invest in buildings that will produce a positive cash flow immediately.

Start Your Own Full or Part-time Business

The last tax shelter, and one I consider the best for black women is starting your own business. It's time black women started working for themselves. Since many of us are hitting the glass ceiling and are not being promoted into upper management, let's get out and start our own companies where we can become the CEO. There are many benefits. First, you control your income and level of opportunity, second, there are tax benefits, and third you can create jobs for today's unemployed black youth.

The United States encourages entrepreneurship by providing tax breaks to those who take the risk. Write-offs such as Keogh retirement plans, cost and depreciation of business equipment, health care premiums, and other business expenses are deductible and can reduce your taxable income dramatically. Starting your own business is the number one best way to become financially independent.

■ NOTES

_____

_____

_____

_____

_____

_____

_____

_____

_____

_____

CHAPTER 12

SAVING STRATEGIES

Your Savings Program

Before you start your investment program there are certain financial basics you need to have in place. This is called "Having Your House in Order." You do not want to risk investing your hard earned dollars unless you are in a financial position to do so. Two of the basics, debt/credit card management and an insurance program, have already been discussed. The last requirement is having a savings program. Studies show that American people save less than 4% of their gross income compared to the Japanese who save 15% or more. In 1995, the average Japanese family saved $86,250.

African Americans save even less—a mere 2%. A major reason for this is that black Americans tend to earn less. But in spite of this we still need to save more. But how, you might ask? The simplest solution is to pay yourself first, there is no other way. On the first and the fifteenth when you are paying your bills, write the first check to yourself. Your goal should be 10% of your monthly net income (after tax). If that is too much, then start lower. Even $10 a month is a start. The key is to start and continue every

month until you reach 10%. You'll soon find you were able to live comfortably without the money, and it's a nice feeling knowing you have a safe cushion to fall back on. Disciplined saving can provide a comfortable retirement, pay for your child's education, buy a home and take that great vacation you have always wanted.

Your savings goal is to first accumulate 3 to 6 months of monthly living expenses. This is your emergency fund. It is used only for emergencies and placed in an area where it is safe and liquid (easy to get to). Savings account choices will be discussed later. After you have your emergency cash fund in place, any additional cash savings is for your investment program and your short term goals.

If you find it too difficult to get into the habit of saving, there are alternatives. Many banks, savings and loans, credit unions, and mutual funds offer automatic monthly deposit from your checking account into a type of savings plan. You tell them the amount you want taken out, the date and where to send it, and they do it for you. You never even see it leave, until you receive your bank statement. If you choose this method, remember to deduct the amount every month from your check register or you'll be bouncing checks everywhere. Many employers offer company savings plans. Here, a portion of your paycheck is automatically deducted and placed in an interest bearing account. If you choose this option, check with your employer on how accessible the money is if needed. Many plans require you to leave the money in for a certain length of time before it can be withdrawn. This won't help you if you need it for an emergency.

Use Time to Your Advantage

Reaching your objective of financial independence takes time and doesn't happen overnight. The key is to use time to your advantage. If you have only a small amount to invest and you are young, you have the ingredients essential to becoming financially independent. With the benefit of time, a small amount soon compounds to a large sum. A savings of $100 per month started at the age of 30, over a 10 year period at an interest rate of 10% adds up to a sum of $20,161. And the higher the interest rate, the faster it adds up (as indicated in **Figure 12-1**).

The power of compounding is phenomenal. With it your dollars can become millions. Look at **Figure 12-2**. If your goal is to save $100,000 by the time you reach 65 and you begin saving at the age of 30, you can reach it by saving $335 per month as long as you can obtain a 10% rate of re-turn. If you wait until you are 45 years old, you will need to save $1,587 per month. The power of compounding with time and the amount of your interest rate are powerful tools to assist you on the road to financial independence. The step you must take is to make a commitment to yourself to save monthly and place the money in an interest bearing account that pays a high rate of return and leave the rest to the power of compounding.

Rule of 72

Of great importance to an investor is the **"Rule of 72."** It will tell you how long it will take to double your money at various interest rates. The formula is to divide the amount of interest rate by 72, e.g., 18% / 72 = 9 years. So if you invest $100 at 8% in 9 years it will become $200. The higher the interest rate the faster it doubles. (See **Figure 12-3** which shows various interest rates and the number of years it will take to double).

The Married Woman's Nest Egg

This is a topic rarely discussed in financial planning books but is very important for women. If you are a married woman, regardless of whether you work outside or in the home, you must have your own savings account in your name only. With today's increased divorce rate and the judicial system not acting in women's favor, more women than ever are literally finding themselves out on the street with children to support and no means of financial support after a divorce. Having your own savings account provides a cushion for you to fall back on. Many women ask, should I keep my savings account a secret from my spouse? The answer is different for everyone. It depends on your relationship, the personality of your spouse, and how well you communicate with each other. If you believe your spouse will feel threatened, then forgo telling him. Otherwise, it isn't necessary to keep it a secret, just make sure you have your nest egg.

The best way to start is by setting aside a small amount of your monthly income, whether it's a paycheck or your grocery money. *Do not and I repeat, do not stash it away in a cookie jar or under your bed*. It is to be placed in an interest bearing account such as a money market mutual fund, where it will earn interest and grow.

This is an important task that married women cannot overlook. There have been too many cases of the wife putting her husband through medical or law school, raising their four children and sacrificing her career and then later, after his graduation the husband leaves her with the children and protests paying a decent alimony and child support.

You want to continue to have a joint savings account with your spouse, but unfortunately times have changed and it is necessary for you to look out for yourself financially and have your own account.

What to Look for in a Savings Account

When shopping around for a place to store your savings you should consider four criteria:

- **Safety**—The last thing you want to do is to lose your hard earned money. The account should have 100% certainty that the principal (the original amount) will not fluctate (go lower). If the value goes up and down, based upon the stock or bond market, then stay away. You could lose money with this investment if there is an emergency and the stock or bond market is down.

  Avoid savings institutions who offer abnormally high rates. Many of these institutions are having financial difficulties and are offering unusually high rates to get you in the door. With the savings and loans currently in a tailspin, check their financial stability carefully. In spite of the FSLIC, Federal Savings & Loan Insurance Corp. and FDIC, Federal Deposit Insurance Corp., which is the government insurance program that protects each account up to $100,000, if a bank is in trouble, it could be a while before you receive your money.

- **Convenience**—Your savings account should offer you a convenient way to save and obtain your money when needed. Stay away from financial institutions that require you to write a letter 30 days in advance. It's your money and you should be

Saving $100 per Month

	5 yrs	10 yrs	15 yrs	20 yrs	25 yrs	30 yrs	35 yrs	40 yrs
5%	$6,810	$15,502	$26,595	$40,754	$58,823	$81,886	$111,319	$148,885
6%	$6,984	$16,331	$28,839	$45,577	$67,977	$97,953	$138,068	$191,750
7%	$7,163	$17,208	$31,298	$51,060	$78,776	$117,651	$172,174	$248,645
8%	$7,345	$18,137	$33,994	$57,294	$91,528	$141,830	$215,740	$324,337
9%	$7,532	$19,120	$36,951	$64,385	$106,595	$171,543	$271,472	$425,225
10%	$7,723	$20,161	$40,192	$72,453	$124,409	$208,084	$342,845	$559,878
11%	$7,919	$21,262	$43,746	$81,634	$145,476	$253,054	$434,329	$739,789
12%	$8,119	$22,427	$47,643	$92,083	$170,401	$308,423	$551,666	$980,343
13%	$8,324	$23,660	$51,916	$103,976	$199,893	$376,614	$702,210	$1,302,100
14%	$8,534	$24,964	$56,600	$117,513	$234,794	$460,610	$895,399	$1,732,547
15%	$8,748	$26,344	$61,736	$132,921	$276,099	$564,082	$1,143,318	$2,308,370

Figure 12-1 Saving $100 Per Month

able to get to it when necessary, not at the convenience of the institution.

- **Liquidity**—Liquidity is being able to cash in your investment as soon as possible. Your savings should be in an account where it can be withdrawn at any time. Don't invest your savings in real estate, antiques, and other collectibles. It takes too much time to sell these investments and usually time is what you don't have.
- **Income**—The objective of your savings is to grow by earning income that is com-

pounded daily, monthly or annually. Do not invest your savings where the income is withheld until sometime late in the future when it matures, such as a zero-coupon bond.

Savings Account Choices

A variety of saving accounts meet these criteria: passbook savings, certificates of de-

Power of Compounding: Annual Investment Required to Reach $100,000.00

Interest Rate	Years							
	5	**10**	**15**	**20**	**25**	**30**	**35**	**40**
5%	17,236.00	7,572.00	4,414.00	2,880.00	1,966.00	1,433.00	1,054.00	788.39
6%	16,736.00	7,157.00	4,053.00	2,565.00	1,720.00	1,193.00	846.59	609.58
7%	16,254.00	6,764.00	3,719.00	2,280.00	1,478.00	989.39	676.08	468.14
8%	15,783.00	6,392.00	3,410.00	2,024.00	1,267.00	817.36	537.34	357.42
9%	15,332.00	6,039.00	3,124.00	1,793.00	1,083.00	673.06	425.31	271.52
10%	14,890.00	5,704.00	2,861.00	1,587.00	924.37	552.66	335.43	205.40
11%	14,467.00	5,388.00	2,618.00	1,403.00	787.41	452.67	263.74	154.84
12%	14,055.00	5,088.00	2,395.00	1,239.00	669.64	369.97	206.41	116.40
13%	13,658.00	4,805.00	2,190.00	1,070.00	568.67	301.83	168.00	87.29
14%	13,270.00	4,536.00	2,001.00	963.69	482.32	245.86	126.47	65.36
15%	12,898.00	4,283.00	1,828.00	848.82	408.64	200.02	98.68	48.88

Ex. By Investing $924.37 per year earning an interest rate of 10% in 25 years you would have a total of $100,000.

Figure 12-2 Power of Compounding

posit, money market mutual funds, and U.S. Treasury bills, notes and bonds. The following is an analysis of each.

Passbook Savings

Of the 4 accounts this is the least desirable. Passbook savings accounts can be found at most banks and savings and loan institu-tions. They pay 2 to 5½% interest, which is way below what your money could be earning. Many financial institutions now charge a service fee for their savings accounts if the balance falls below a set minimum in which case your total return would be less than 2%.

Rule of 72

Rate of Return	4%	6%	8%	10%	12%
Years	$1,000	$1,000	$1,000	$1,000	$1,000
6					$2,000
7.2				$2,000	
9			$2,000		
12		$2,000			
14.4				$4,000	
18	$2,000		$2,000		$8,000
21.6				$8,000	
24		$4,000			$16,000
27			$8,000		
28.8				$16,000	
30					$32,000
Final Amount (36 Years)	$4,000	$8,000	$16,000	$32,000	$64,000

Example: 12% rate of return, your $1,000 will double in 6 years.

Figure 11-2 Rule of 72

Money Market Deposit Accounts

This is the only bank account that offers safety, liquidity, and money market yields. It is federally insured up to $100,000 and the bank usually requires a minimum balance of $1,000 to $2,500. The two disadvantages are that you can write only three checks a month and the interest rate earns less than money market mutual funds. This account is for you only if you can maintain the minimum balance and absolutely must have the federal insurance.

Certificates of Deposit CDs

These are offered by most banks and savings and loans. They are for people who will not need their money right away. Maturities range from 30 days to 5 years. The most common are 3 months, 6 months, 1 year and 18 months. A minimum deposit of $500 or $1,000 is required. CDs are also insured up to $100,000 through FDIC and FSLIC.

The interest rate is fixed throughout the term of the certificate and the amount you receive depends upon how long you tie the money up. The longer you tie it up the higher the rate. If the funds are withdrawn early, before the maturity date, the penalty charge varies from 1 to 3 months of interest depending on the term of the CDs. If interest rates are going up, invest in short term CDs; 6 months or less. If rates are declining, consider 12 months or longer.

Money Market Mutual Fund

The best place for your savings is the money market mutual fund. This is an account offered by mutual fund companies, usually one of many funds they offer. The minimum initial investment ranges from $1,000 to $5,000. There is no cost to put money in or to take out. Money market mutual funds differ from stock and bond mutual funds in that they invest in low-risk cash equivalents, such as government and corporate paper.

The interest on money market mutual funds fluctuates and compounds daily. The rate is usually ½ to 1% higher than the bank money market deposit account, and tends to keep up with inflation. If interest rates are rising, the rate of interest will increase. The opposite can also happen. If rates are decreasing your money market rate decreases. But even then it is usually paying much more than the banks and savings and loan.

Unlike the bank accounts, the money market mutual funds are not federally insured. But the investments the funds buys are so safe that the chance of losing are practically nil.

The easiest access to your money is through check writing. Most money market mutual funds allow unlimited check writing as long as the checks are $500 or more. If you are in the upper tax bracket and live in a state with high income taxes such as California, New York, and Massachusetts, you can earn more with tax-free money market fund. The interest rate is lower but you do not have to pay taxes on the interest income.

Tax-free money market funds invest in short-term money market instruments which are issued by municipalities and state governments. The interest is exempt from federal taxes. If you invest in a tax-free money market fund that is issued by the state in which you reside, state tax is also exempt. You should only consider tax-free money funds if you are in the 28 to 39.6% tax bracket.

Other Saving Alternatives

U.S. Treasury Bills

These are safe securities which are issued and backed by the federal government. The income from treasury securities is exempt from state and local taxes, not federal. Treasury bills have 3 month, 6 month, and 1 year maturities. The minimum investment is $10,000 with $5,000 increments. They are sold at a discount and redeemed at face value on maturity. You can purchase these through the Federal Reserve Bank free of charge or through a stockbroker or a bank for a fee of $25 or $50. They are somewhat liquid in that they can be sold prior to their maturity date, but at the market rate, which can be either higher or lower than the original investment. The yield on treasury bills fluctuates.

U.S. Treasury Notes

U.S. Treasury notes have longer maturities which range from 1 to 10 years. The rate is fixed and interest is paid twice a year. Notes with maturities of 4 years or longer are available for a minimum of $1,000; for shorter maturities, the minimum is $5,000. Because the maturities are longer, selling these bonds before maturity can be a problem. If interest rates have gone up and your note is yielding below the current market value, selling early means a possible loss of our principal (original investment). The yield on treasury notes is lower than their corporate counterpart because of the safety rating of the U.S. Government.

U.S. Treasury Bonds

U.S. Treasury bonds have even longer maturities of 10 to 30 years. They can be purchased for $1,000 and also pay interest income twice a year. As with treasury notes, selling these bonds before maturity can result in loss of principal. Because of the longer maturities, U.S. Treasury notes and bonds are not recommended for your emergency money.

Summary

Saving regularly is the only means of reaching your goal of financial independence. You must start a savings program *today* by either paying yourself first or having the money deducted automatically from your paycheck.

A savings account will contribute to your feeling more abundant and self sufficient and that, in return, will attract more money to you. Having savings will give you options and freedom in life that you would not otherwise have. You will have greater control over your financial future as well as having the freedom and power to do good for your community. You don't need a fortune to start. With the effects of compounding, a small amount saved regularly can become a large amount in no time.

If you are married, make sure you have your own savings account separate from your joint account. It isn't that you don't trust or love your spouse, but these times require black women to take on more financial responsibilities than before.

There are many options available for your savings money. Be sure to compare interest rates, safety and the length of time the money must be held in the account. You want the highest rate but of utmost importance is that you cannot lose your original investment. You also want to be able to get to it immediately in case of an emergency.

■ NOTES

_____

_____

_____

_____

_____

_____

_____

_____

_____

_____

CHAPTER 13

PLANNING FOR YOUR CHILDREN'S EDUCATION

In the black community, educating our youth ranks as the number one priority to best meet the challenges of the twenty-first century. As we move from an industrial to an informational society many young black Americans lack sufficient educational and technological skills to obtain jobs that enable them to function properly in this society. Youth are hit hardest by unemployment in the black community.

If black Americans want to obtain equal status in this society we must control our own wealth and income. This can be achieved by parents encouraging their children to obtain the best possible education.

A good education is expensive, but the value for personal growth and future success is enormous. A college diploma is the ticket you need to obtain a well-paying and exciting career.

The high cost of college has hindered many black youths from attending college, particularly with the sharp cut-backs of financial aid programs. And the future looks even bleaker. College costs are expected to increase at an average rate of 7% per year for the next 20 years. And financial aid is expected to decrease even more. A 4 year college education could cost approximately $50,000 at a public college and $100,000 at a private college.

Cost of College in the Next Decade

Below are 10 well known institutions and their average cost for tuition, fees, room and board, personal expenses, and transportation for 1 year:

	1996
1. Howard University	12,498
2. Spelman College	13,591
3. Morehouse College	14,150
4. Tuskegee University	10,837
5. Harvard University	22,417
6. Princeton University	21,933
7. U.C.L.A	18,058
8. Yale University	29,029
9. Stanford University	27,403
10. Georgetown University	28,580

As staggering as these figures are, college aid specialists believe these costs could double in the twenty-first century.

Figure 13-1 shows the future cost of college with an inflation rate of 7%.

Saving for College

Developing a college savings plan isn't as hopeless as you might think. I always believe where there's a will there's a way. The key is to start early and save regularly when your children are young. If you don't have a lot of extra income left over at the end of the month, that's okay. Start with a small amount each month and raise it every time your income increases. By putting away just $50 a month into an investment earning 8% annually, your child's nest egg would be worth $17,417 at the end of 15 years.

Paying for college is a lot like buying a house. The more you save now for the down payment, the less you'll have to borrow or pay out-of-pocket later. So the sooner you start putting money aside for college, the better off you'll be.

What's the Best Way to Save?

The custodial account is one of the more popular methods to save for college. It is set up and managed by an adult for the benefit of a minor. The account is listed in the name and social security number of the child. Any money put in the account belongs to the child and is an irrevocable gift (you can't take it back). As the custodian of the account, you manage the money until your child reaches the age of majority (18 or 21 depending on the state law governing the custodial account).

This account also allows for tax savings. If your child is under the age of 14, the first $600 of investment income is tax free, the next $600 is taxed at the child's rate (usually 15%). Any income above $1,200 is taxed at the parent's rate. Once your child reaches 14, the first $600 is free of federal taxes, and any amount over that is taxed at the child's rate.

This account also allows parents or grandparents to give gifts of property or cash to minors. You are allowed to give $10,000 ($20,000 if given jointly with your spouse) to each child annually without a gift tax.

While this is a great way to build your child's nest egg, it has its potential problems. When your child reaches the age of majority, he or she gains complete control over the assets in the account. If he or she decides to buy a Porsche instead of attending Howard University, I'm afraid there's nothing you can do.

You may also wreck your child's chances of getting financial aid from a college or the government. That's because children must contribute 35% of their own savings toward college costs each year before they qualify for financial aid. If the savings account is in the parent's name, the formula states they need only contribute 5.6% of their personal savings. The solution: save your child's college money in your name, that way you'll continue to have control over the money if your child decides not to go to college. If she does decide to, she may qualify for financial aid.

The other way to save for college is to set up an irrevocable living trust. With this type of plan, which you must set up with an attorney, you can specify how much money will be distributed to your child and at what time period. These trusts are beneficial in certain circumstances but can have complex tax ramifications. You should consult an attorney before considering this choice.

How Much Should I Save?

The answer to this question is very difficult to answer unless you know which college your child will attend and its future cost.

There are 3 college building plans currently offered by major financial institutions that will assist you in figuring how much you need to save: College Savings Bank of Princeton, New Jersey (1-800-888-2723), Fidelity Investments (1-800-544-6666), and Merrill Lynch (call local office). You give the plan the age of your child and the school he or she may attend and they will send a computer printout of the amount you need to save annually. The service is free and each institution usually recommends you invest in their investments. For more infor-

mation you can contact them at the numbers above.

What Are Your Options— Financial Aid?

For financial aid look first for scholarships and grants. These are gifts of money that don't have to be repaid. Scholarships are usually based on achievement and grants are based on need. Both private organizations and the federal government make several scholarships and grants available for African Americans.

Two excellent books addressing scholarships and grants through private organizations are the Directory of Financial Aid for Minorities, and Directory of Financial Aid for Women, both written by Gail Ann Schlachter and available in most main libraries. The scholarships and grants range in amount from $300 to $2,500. Individual colleges also sponsor scholarships and grants. You must check with the school your child applies to.

The federal government currently sponsors two major grant programs, **Pell grants** and the **Supplemental Educational Opportunity grants**. The Pell grant program is the largest federal aid program. Grants range from $200 to $2,300 per year, are based on need, and typically go to families with incomes less than $30,000 per year.

Awarded to undergraduates, the Supplemental Education Opportunity grant supplements the Pell grant, gives the money

Annual College Cost in the Future with an Inflation Rate of 7%

Child Age	Year Child Will Enter College	Four-Year Public College Resident Student	Four-Year Private College Resident Student
18	1996	$ 6,709	$ 12,194
17	1997	7,179	13,048
16	1998	7,682	13,961
15	1999	8,220	14,938
14	2000	8,795	15,984
13	2001	9,411	17,103
12	2002	10,070	18,300
11	2003	10,775	19,581
10	2004	11,529	20,952
9	2005	12,336	22,419
8	2006	13,200	23,988
7	2007	14,124	25,667
6	2008	15,113	27,464
5	2009	16,171	29,386
4	2010	17,303	31,443
3	2011	18,514	33,644
2	2012	19,810	35,999
1	2013	21,197	38,519

Figure 13-1 Annual College Cost

directly to the college, and the college distributes it to students with needs of their choice. The awards range from $200 to $4,000 per year.

The second category of financial aid includes work study, co-operative education, and the military.

Work Study

The federal government currently sponsors a college work study program that provides money to colleges to employ needy full and part-time students with jobs, usually on campus and at minimum wage. The money is paid directly to the students. Studies have shown that students in this type of program have better grade point averages than students who do not work, since they must budget their time more carefully.

Co-Operative Education

Co-operative education is a program consisting of a combination of school and employment. Unlike the work study program it is a 5 to 6 year program where in the first year the student takes the basic courses in her major. The next 4 to 5 years are spent alternating quarters of work and study. The advantages of the program are that the student earns most of her tuition and, in addition, has 2 or more years of career related work experience. Such experience leads often to job offers after graduation from the employing companies. Not all colleges offer this program. For additional information,

write to: The National Commission for Co-Operative Education, 360 Huntingdon Ave. Boston, MA 02115.

Military Services

The military has become a large financier of college educational aid. Every branch of the armed forces and military academies such as West Point or the coast guard offer scholarship programs for students who are academically qualified. The scholarships pay for tuition, room and board, books, plus a monthly stipend ranging from $140 to $480. After graduation students are required to serve 4 to 6 years in the military branch offering the scholarship.

College Loans

The final category and currently the most used financial aid package is college loans. These must be repaid, are available from the individual colleges, and are subsidized and guaranteed by the federal or state government.

These are three major federally guaranteed loans, 1) **Stafford loan**, 2) **Perkins loan** and 3) **Plus loan** (parent loan for undergraduate students).

Formerly called the Federal Guaranteed Student loan, the Stafford loan is available to all college undergraduates and graduate students and is based on need. The maximum loan is $2,625 a year for first and second year students, $4,000 for third and fourth year students and $7,500 for graduate students. The current interest on the loan starts at 8% annually and rises to 10% in the fourth year of repayment. A student has up to 10 years after graduation to pay back the loan.

The Perkins loan, formerly the National Direct Student loan, are loans given directly to accredited colleges by the federal government to distribute to undergraduate and graduate students. The loans are based on need and the student can borrow from $4,500 for a 2 year program to $9,000 for a 4 year program. At 5%, the interest rate is low and repayment must begin 9 months after graduation with 10 years to complete.

Plus loans (parent loan for undergraduate students), can be obtained by parents or students and do not require a family to demonstrate financial need. As long as you have a clean credit rating you can receive a loan up to $4,000 a year. The interest rate varies and floats at 3.25 percentage points above a 1 year treasury bill rate. The lender can raise or lower it once a year and it cannot exceed 12%. Repayment of Plus loans must begin 60 days after the money is received and must be repaid within 10 years.

For more information and advice about federal loan and grant programs, consult The College Cost Book (The College Board $12.95), an excellent resource guide available at local book stores.

Other Creative Financing Alternatives

Since interest on student loans is no longer deductible, you may get the best college financing deal by taking out a home equity loan or borrowing against your life insurance policy.

Home equity loans have recently become major sources of money for college due to tax reform. Currently the law states that interest on home equity loans is fully deductible on loans up to $100,000. The interest rate is usually variable and 2 to 3 percentage points above treasury bill rate.

Most financial institutions will allow you to borrow 70 to 80% of your equity (which is the house's market value minus the unpaid balance on your first mortgage.) One danger to avoid before borrowing: The bank which lends you the money uses your home as collateral for the repayment of the loan, if you fail to make the loan payments you could lose your home.

If you've been paying on a whole-life insurance policy for a long time most likely you have built up a "cash value." Most life insurance policies have a provision for you to borrow up to 80% of the cash value without a specific repayment time limit. The interest is generally very low ranging from 5 to 10%. The amount borrowed is reduced from your insurance coverage until the loan is repaid. Therefore if you have a $10,000 policy and you borrow $5,000 and do not repay the loan, in case of your death, the beneficiary will receive only $5,000 instead of $10,000. So before you borrow, make sure you have other adequate insurance protection.

Investments for Your College Funds

Saving for college is just like saving for your retirement. Since the bulk of college financial aid is now dependent on you, the type of savings and investment plan you choose is of the utmost importance.

Your investment strategy for the money placed in a college fund should be based on the age of your children. When they are young, place the bulk of the money in stocks, which tend to outperform other investments over the long haul. Try not to worry about the occasional down years, the up years will more than make up for them. When your children are older, place the money in investments that are less risky.

Children Newborn to Twelve

Invest college money into mutual funds that buy growth oriented stocks. Have the mutual fund set up your account in the automatic investing plan where you can invest $50 to $100 every month, regardless of the changes in the stock market. You can even request that the money be taken directly from your payroll check or out of your checking or savings account, making it a painless way to save.

Children Twelve to Fourteen

College is just around the corner, so this is the time when you need to be more conser-vative with your investments. You want to gradually shift out of the stock mutual funds and into fixed investments such as long-term certificates of deposits, zero coupon bonds that mature when your child starts school and series EE bonds. These investments will not fluctuate like stocks, therefore avoiding the risk that the money will not be available when your child starts college. Maintain at least 50% of the money in the mutual fund so that it will continue to grow and keep up with inflation.

Children 14 and Over

Your college money should not be invested in any investments where the principal is at risk, i.e. the stock market. Instead, keep the money absolutely safe by investing in short-term treasury securities whose interest is state tax free, and certificates of deposit.

Help from the Government

Recognizing the burden parents are facing in paying for their children's education, several states have begun issuing college savings bonds which are similar to tax-free zero coupon bonds. Not all states offer these bonds. Check with your stockbroker or financial planner for availability in your state. Many states are proposing new legislation and tax breaks for parents financing college educa-tion. Expect to see positive changes soon.

College Costs Worksheet

Tuition	$_____
Room and Board	$_____
Books	$_____
Transportation	$_____
Personal Expenses	$_____
Clothing	$_____
Laundry	$_____
Recreation	$_____
Medical and Dental Expenses	$_____
Fraternity/Sorority Expenses	$_____
Emergency Savings	$_____
Miscellaneous	$_____
Total	$_____

Worksheet 13-2 College Costs

■ NOTES

_____

_____

_____

_____

CHAPTER 14

RETIREMENT PLANNING

Start Planning Today

As the twenty-first century approaches, long-term retirement planning for black women is becoming increasingly important. With the help of modern science, people are living a lot longer, particularly women. Studies are proving that a 65-year-old female today has a life expectancy of another 20 years. So where will the money you need to live on come from? Don't plan on social security. By the time you are ready to retire it may not be there. Or the amount you will receive could be very small. It will be up to you to obtain the bulk of the money, ideally, through a combination of savings, private pension funds, insurance and social security.

The *"graying of America"* is a description of our future according to the latest Census Bureau. A large percentage of this rapidly growing group can expect to live in poverty or very close to it.

According to the latest Census Bureau report, over 41% of black women age 65 and over live in poverty, with incomes of less than $5,000 and 50% of it is from social security. This percentage of black women in poverty is substantially higher than that of white and Hispanic women. No longer can you depend on the government to provide for you during your golden years nor should you wait until you are in your fifties and sixties to start saving for it. Start planning today. The sooner you begin, the better your chances of reaching financial independence by your retirement years. It all boils down to taking the responsibility and having the discipline to start a retirement plan.

How Much Money Will I Need? A lot.

African-American women are not saving nearly enough money to live comfortably in retirement. If you think you'll be able to live the good life with social security, forget it. Study after study shows there will be so many people needing benefits the government will have to reduce benefits to make the available money go around. The money you receive from social security will only take care of one third of your living expenses. The rest will be up to you.

How much money you need to ensure a comfortable retirement depends on what you

How Much Money Will I Need

	Example	You
Annual Retirement Needs		
1. Enter your estimated annual retirement expenses (80% of current income).	$32,000	_____
2. Enter the total amount you will receive annually from your pension and social security	$20,000	_____
3. The amount you will need annually in retirement from personal savings. (Subtract line 2 from line 1.)	$12,000	_____
Your Retirement Savings Goal		
4. At what age do you plan to retire? Select the age and enter the factor from the table below.	17.4	_____

Retirement Age	55	60	62	65	67	70
Factor	21.5	19.6	18.8	17.4	16.4	14.9

	Example	You
5. The amount you will need to save to retire at 65. (Multiply line 3 by line 4.)	$208,800	_____
If You Plan to Retire Early		
6. If you want to retire before the age of 65, select the rate and enter the factor from the table below.	8.5	_____

Retirement Age	55	60	62
Factor	8.5	4.6	2.8

	Example	You
7. The additional money you will need to retire early. (Multiply line 2 by line 6.)	$170,000	_____
8. Total savings needed by your desired retirement age. (Add lines 5 and 7.)	$378,800	_____
Money Already Saved		
9. Enter the money you've already saved. Include 401(k), profit-sharing plans, savings, investments, and IRAs.	$20,000	_____
10. How many years remain before you retire? Enter the factor from the table below.	1.80	_____

Years before retirement	5	10	15	20	25	30	35
Factors		1.22	1.48	1.80	2.19	2.67	3.24	3.95

	Example	You
11. Value of your savings at the time you retire. (Multiply line 9 by line 10.)	$36,000	_____
Annual Savings to Meet Your Goal		
12. Enter the amount you still need in addition to your savings. (Subtract line 11 line from line 8.)	$342,800	_____
13. Enter the factor from the table below for the number of years until retirement.	.049	_____

Years until retirement	5	10	15	20	25	30	35
Factors		.184	.083	.049	.033	.024	.017	.013

	Example	You
14. Amount you need to save each year to retire. (Multiply line 12 by line 13.)	$16,797	_____

Worksheet 14-1 How Much Money Will You Need?
Source: Charles Schwab, T. Rowe Price

expect of life after retirement. If you're like me, you probably are looking forward to a better life during your retirement. You may want to travel more, start a new hobby, or pursue an old one. But these activities take money, and having money takes planning.

The rule of thumb to calculate how much money you will need during your retirement years is that your retirement income should be 80% of your current income, adjusted for inflation: You must take a realistic look at your current day-to-day expenses and figure out how much you can expect to get from your company pension plan (if you have one), 401(k) or 403(b) plan, social security, and your personal savings.

For a quick estimate of how much money you will need, take a look at **Worksheet 14-1**. To complete the form properly you will need to obtain in advance an estimate of (1) your annual pension benefits from your employer, and (2) your annual social security benefits from the social security Administration office (1-800-772-1213).

On the worksheet, I have included the retirement calculations of a 40-year-old single black woman making $40,000 a year who wants to retire at age 55. She will need a nest egg of $378,000 in order to maintain a decent standard of living. As you can see, the money she already has saved is far from the needed amount. For her to reach her goal, she will need to save $16,797 annually for the next 15 years.

If you're planning to improve your lifestyle during your retirement years, estimate what your new annual expenses will be and use that figure instead of 80% of your current income. It's always better to overestimate when planning for your retirement.

Social Security, Will It Be There When I Need It?

Yes, social security will probably still be around. The major question is, will it be enough to live on during retirement? The answer to that is definitely no. And you most likely will not get back from social security as much money as you will have put in through your payroll taxes.

Social security retirement benefits were never intended to replace all your lost earnings. They were to provide a base and to supplement your savings, pensions, investment, insurance and other income. Unfortunately, many retirees today depend largely on social security benefits. And since there is a "graying of America," nearly twice as many people by the year 2000 are expected to be collecting social security checks.

Due to these projections the government has already started to make changes in the social security benefits. Starting in the year 2000, you will have to retire later in order to receive full benefits. Currently the age to receive full benefits is 65, by the year 2005, the minimum age will reach 66 and stay there until 2016. The age will be hiked annually until the year 2027 when it will reach the maximum age of 67. But there is new talk of increasing the age even further. The 76 million baby boomers (people born between 1946 and 1964) are expected to live far longer than today's retirees because of medical advances and also because many have adopted healthier lifestyles. This large increase in retirees would overwhelm the social security system.

If you retire later, the government will reward you by enlarging your social security check by 3 to 8% for each year between the age of 65 and 70 you delay taking full benefits. If you decide to retire early you'll receive less money.

More of your social security income will become taxable. The law presently states that retirees have to pay taxes on up to 85% of their social security income if their other income from investments, savings, etc. plus half of social security exceeds $32,000 for married couples filing a joint return and $25,000 for single people. When calculating whether or not your social security income is taxable you will also have to include any tax-free interest you receive from municipal bonds.

Your social security payroll tax (FICA) is now higher. The rates have been raised so high they not only pay for today's retirees but are also building a surplus to pay for future retirees as well.

How Social Security Is Earned

The amount of money you receive in social security income is based on a number of factors: The number of years you have worked, your annual income and the age you start collecting the social security income. You can write to your local Social Security office to obtain an estimate figure of your future benefits. You can safely count on an average social security income equal to 10 to 20% of your pre-retirement salary.

Should I Invest in an IRA— Individual Retirement Account?

There are a number of options available for starting your retirement planning. Those providing the fastest growth are the tax-deferred accounts such as an IRA or your employee savings plan where you are able to earn income on the money and pay no income taxes until you withdraw it.

Although the 1986 Tax Reform Act changed the deductibility rules for Individual Retirement Accounts, an IRA remains a vital element for your retirement planning and can help you achieve your retirement goals.

In 1981, the IRA was available to every person under the age of $70\frac{1}{2}$ with earned income. You were able to contribute 100% of your annual earned income up to $2,000, and deduct that amount from your taxable income. The income from the account was allowed to grow tax deferred until you reached the age of $59\frac{1}{2}$ and began withdrawing, at which time you would pay taxes. If both husband and wife worked each could contribute $2,000 to an IRA account and deduct $4,000 from their taxable income. And if there was an unemployed spouse, $2,250 could be contributed and deducted. Before Tax Reform 1986 IRA's provided the best of both worlds. You were able to save on income taxes and save for your retirement.

Tax Reform 1986, still permits you, if you are under the age of 70½, to contribute the lesser of 100% of earned income or $2,000 to an IRA, and $2,250 if you have a un-employed spouse. The difference is that if you or your spouse are active participants in an employer sponsored retirement plan and your adjusted gross income (after deductions) is above a specific level, the amount of the contribution that can be deducted from your taxable income is gradually phased out or eliminated.

If you are single, an active participant in your employer's retirement plan and have adjusted gross income of less than $25,000 you can contribute $2,000 to your IRA and still deduct it from your taxable income. If you are married filing a joint tax return and you, your spouse, or both are active participants in a plan, your adjusted gross income (AGI) must be less than $40,000 in order to deduct the full $2,000 from your taxable income. As your income rises, the deduction phases out. No deduction is allowed to a married couple with AGI of $50,000 or a single person with AGI of $35,000.

If you or your spouse is not active in an employee retirement plan you can contribute and deduct up to the $2,000 limit. If married, filing jointly, both parties cannot be involved in a plan in order to take advantage of the deduction.

The one continuing advantage of the IRA, is that the earnings, gains or dividends grow without taxes until you begin to receive the distribution. This compounded tax-deferred growth allows you to save for retirement faster and more profitably than you could if taxes were paid each year. See **Figure 14-2**.

Your IRA is for retirement and if money is withdrawn from the account before the age of 59½, you must pay a 10% penalty plus taxes on the original amount plus interest if you were able to deduct or just on the earnings if you did not deduct. So if you think you will need the money sooner and still want to save for retirement there are alternatives. You can invest each year in tax-free municipal bonds or a municipal bond fund instead of an IRA, promising yourself to withdraw the money only at retirement or for an emergency. This way, if the money is needed, you avoid the 10% penalty. With this method you also need the discipline to stick with your promise and not touch the money unless absolutely necesary.

If you are going to contribute to an IRA, there are 2 important factors you must consider in order to make your IRA beneficial. The first is the time of the year to make your IRA contribution. No matter whether it is deductible or not, you should make your IRA contribution early in the year. Don't wait until April 15 of the following year. By investing early, you give your money more time to begin growing tax deferred. Over time, this can make a substantial difference in the value of your IRA because of the compounding. For example, over the course of 30 years, $2,000 with annual return of

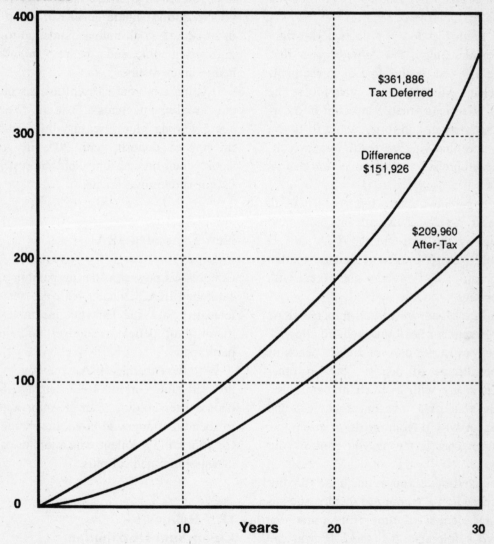

IRA Taxable vs. Tax Deferred Accumulation

$ In Thousands

$361,886
Tax Deferred

Difference
$151,926

$209,960
After-Tax

400

300

200

100

0

10   **Years**   20   30

The chart above shows after 30 years there may be 72% more in the tax-deferred IRA than in a taxable account.

Figure 14-2 IRA Taxable vs Tax-Deferred Accumulation

10% invested at the beginning rather than the end of the year will increase the worth of your account by $35,000. So the earlier the contribution the better.

The second factor, is selecting the right investment strategy. The value of your IRA will be affected by the type of investments you select. No longer can you invest the money in a money market account or a certificate of deposit and forget about it. If you do, by the time you are ready to retire, inflation will probably have eroded most of its value.

There are now many types of IRAs to choose from. The most advantageous and versatile is the self-directed IRA and is available through brokerage houses, mutual funds, banks, and savings and loans with various fees.

The key advantage of self-directed IRAs is the investment flexibility you are allowed. You can invest not only in savings accounts and certificates of deposit, but in other choices, many with a much higher return. Making your own investment choices and shifting at will if your goals or economic conditions change means you control your money.

The investments you decide upon for your IRA depend on a number of factors, such as your age, length of time from retirement and, your tolerance for risk. If you are younger than 35, you should consider a large portion—70% in growth investments such as stocks and stock mutual funds; 15 to 25% in fixed income such as bonds, certificates of deposit, and money markets; and the re-mainder in inflation hedge investments such as real estate.

If you are in your late thirties and forties, your portfolio should consist of 40 to 50% in stock and stock mutual funds, 30 to 40% in fixed income and, the rest in inflation hedge investments.

If you are in your early fifties, the bulk of your retirement funds—70% in fixed income, Ginnie Maes, treasury bills, and certificates of deposit, with 20% in growth stock, stock mutual funds and the rest in inflation hedge investments.

New Expanded IRA

Congress is now considering passing a new expanded IRA. It finally realized that when it scaled back the IRA tax incentives, the majority of people no longer bothered to participate.

With the expanded IRA, you wouldn't get hit with the current 10% penalty if you chose, after holding your IRA for a while, to spend the money to buy a first home, pay for your child's college education, or pay off catastrophic medical bills.

IRA Rollovers—
Lump Sum Distribution

For the individual who is either retiring early or changing jobs and has vested benefits with the company, you can now take your lump sum and transfer it into an IRA rollover and not be taxed on the distribution. The distribution must be transferred to the IRA rollover account within 60 days from the time it is paid out to you. If you decide to keep some of the money and not roll it over, the amount you do not rollover is subject to taxes and a penalty if you are under 59½.

Just recently, as a disincentive for you to pull money out of this account, the IRS has tacked on an additional tax if you withdraw money from a qualified plan. This penalty is called the 20% withholding tax. The law states that 20% of the rollover amount must be withheld by the plan trustee unless the employee (you) instructs the trustee to transfer the money directly to another eligible retirement plan or IRA. You avoid this withholding tax by not taking possession of the money regardless of the 60 day available rollover period.

The IRA rollover is similar to the IRA account in that the earnings, gains and dividends are compounded tax deferred until you make a withdrawal. If you invest in a self-directed IRA rollover you also have the flexibility of choosing the investments that meet your goals and objectives.

Other Qualified Retirement Plans

401(k)

One of the most attractive retirement plans is the 401(k) employer sponsored retirement plan. This is a plan offered by employers allowing employees to put away part of their paycheck before the money is taxed; thus reducing their tax bill for the current year.

Under the 401(k), you agree to defer part of your income, and the employer puts that deferred pay in a company investment account. As the money accumulates you do not pay taxes on the deferred income nor on the gains and interest the money earns. Also, in many cases the employer will match 25%, 50%, or even 100% of the money you put in, basically doubling your money before it even starts to earn interest.

Here is an example of how a 401(k) works: If you were to earn $35,000 a year and decided to place 5% of your annual income into your company 401(k) and your company matched 100%, your company would match your contribution of $1,750, dollar per dollar, giving you a total of $3,500 in the plan the first year. Your taxable income would also be less because your contribution of $1,750 is deducted leaving you with a taxable income of $33,250.

Under the IRS laws, you can contribute up to $9,240 per year into a 401(k) plan. This figure increases annually adjusted for inflation. The maximum annual combined contribution (you and your employer) cannot exceed 25% of your pay or $30,000 whichever is less, which is considerably more than the $2,000 per year limit on an IRA.

The biggest drawback of the 401(k) plan are the rules regarding withdrawal from the plan. Previously you were able to withdraw from your 401(k) without a 10% penalty before you reached the age of 59½ if you could prove financial hardship. Many people at that time were withdrawing money for tuition, remodeling a home or buying their first home. Now the law is so worded that even if you prove financial hardship you most likely will owe a 10% penalty in addition to the income taxes on the amount you withdraw. The one exception is money used for medical expenses. If these exceed 7½% of your adjusted gross income you will not have to pay the 10% penalty.

A favorable change created by the new tax law for your company 401(k) plan is the length of time it takes to become vested in the plan. Vesting means that you are entitled to receive the company benefits after you leave the company. As of January 1, 1989, you will be 100% vested in the 401(k) company matching plan after 5 years of service instead of 10 years. This is of particular benefit to black women, because so many of us change jobs due to lack of advancement and discrimination that when we terminate our employment we leave a substantial portion of our pension benefits behind, requiring us to start from square one when we obtain a new position with a new company. Now under the new tax law we can take the money with us, and transfer it into an IRA rollover which will continue to shelter it from income taxes.

Where Should I Invest My 401(k) Money?

Once you've taken the step to invest in your company's 401(k) plan, the next decision you must make is how to invest the money. Unfortunately, most employers don't provide you with enough information to make an intelligent decision. The way it usually works is that the company gives you a choice of 5 or more investment options. Among the selections on a typical 401(k) menu are (1) a basic growth-stock mutual fund, (2) a bond fund, (3) an aggressive stock fund, (4) a balanced fund that invests in both stocks and bonds, (5) an international fund, (6) a money market fund, and (7) Guaranteed Interest Contracts (GICs). You can split your money among these options any way you want, and depending on the plan's terms, shift your money around quarterly or even daily.

When you're deciding on which options for your money, there are no hard and fast rules. Factors you want to look at, though, are how close you are to retirement and how much risk you're willing to take. What you don't want to do is invest all our money into the company stock. If the company gets into trouble, you may lose your job as well as your 401(k) money. It's best to avoid putting all your eggs in one company. It's better to spread your money among the options.

But you don't want to invest too conservatively by keeping all your 401(k) money in the money market fund or the Guaranteed Interest Contracts (GICs). These investments pay such low interest you'll never make any money nor will you keep up with inflation. Instead, if you have 30 to 40 years before you retire, it's better to invest heavily where you'll get the most growth—and that's in stocks. In fact, I recommend that you invest 75%–80% of your 401(k) money in the stock mutual fund options. Here's an example of an asset allocation of a 401(k) mutual fund portfolio for a woman with 30 years to go until retirement:

> 40% Growth stocks
> 30% Aggressive growth stocks
> 10% International stocks
> 20% High quality bonds

It isn't necessary to change these allocations until you approach retirement age. But I do suggest you check the performance of your 401(k) by reading the plan's annual statement. If you find one or more of the funds is continually underperforming, you should consider shifting any additional money you add into the plan into the higher performing funds.

Retirement Plans for Non-Profit Institutions

If you work for a non-profit institution such as a school or church, instead of a 401(k) plan you qualify for a tax-sheltered annuity plan called a 403(b). This allows teachers and other employees of non-profit institutions to have as much as 20% to a maximum of $9,500 deducted from their pay checks and placed in a tax-sheltered annuity program offered through a life insurance company or a mutual fund.

Through this plan you are able to avoid paying taxes on the amount you contribute and reduce your taxable income by the amount of the reduction thus lowering your overall tax bill.

Retirement Planning for the Self-Employed

If you are self-employed or have any self-employment income from a moonlighting business, the government has allowed you the opportunity to save for your own retirement. Currently a number of plans are available, some of which are too difficult to explain here and are basically for large corporations. If you have a large company and need more information you should contact a pension plan specialist.

There are 2 plans earmarked for the company with fewer than 25 employees. 1) IRA-Sep and 2) Keoghs. With an IRA-Sep you are allowed to make a maximum contribution of 15% or $30,000 whichever is less of your net self-employment income each year. With the Keogh plan you can contribute up to 20% of your annual net income up to $30,000 whichever is less. In both plans you are able to deduct the contribution from your taxable income for the current tax year, thus lowering your taxable income. Just like an IRA, the gain and interest you receive on your money grows tax deferred until you withdraw it. Your investment options are also open. You can invest the money in treasury bills, stocks, bonds, or real estate limited partnerships. Both plans are available through mutual funds, brokerage houses, financial planners, banks, and insurance companies.

The Power of Compounding

If you want to enjoy your retirement years start planning today. The advantage of starting a savings program early for your retirement or any major financial purchase such as a college education are due to the benefits of compounding. Money earned from regular deposits can grow when allowed to earn interest and compound over the years.

■ **NOTES**

_____

_____

_____

_____

_____

_____

_____

_____

_____

_____

_____

_____

_____

_____

PART 3

INVESTMENT OPPORTUNITIES

CHAPTER 15

BUILDING YOUR INVESTMENT PORTFOLIO

Once you have set your financial goals, saved a 3 to 6 month emergency cash reserve fund, reduced your credit debt, and have adequate total insurance coverage, you can start the most exciting part of reaching financial independence—investing your money.

Investing and developing your investment portfolio is a lifetime process. In order to become a savvy financier you must study a variety of investment vehicles to understand how each will fit into your financial portfolio.

In spite of the stock market crash of 1987, investing your money in the stock market is still one of the best ways to increase our net worth substantially. You will probably make mistakes along the way—that's part of the investment game—but if you work at the rules and acquire some knowledge before parting with your cash, not only will you limit your mistakes, you'll also increase your profit.

Aim of Investing

The aim of investing is to make money through long-term capital growth. Having a powerful investment program will put an end to dependency on others (employers or the government). In the twenty-first century, an investment plan is as essential to your life as a home or automobile. It can be your ticket to financial freedom.

The type of investments you make will depend on your particular goals, the state of the economy and your financial circumstances. You should always be prepared for bear markets—when stock prices are down. It can last for months or years. If your money is needed within the next 2 years then forgo investing in stock or bonds. The market is too volatile for short-term funds and you are much more likely to take a loss by needing to sell too soon. Short-term money should be placed in a money market mutual fund, where the risk of losing your money is extremely low.

What Is Your Investment Objective?

Before beginning your investment program it is important to assess your personal financial situation and decide if you need to concentrate on investing for 1) growth where you receive little or no income but capital appreciation in the future or 2) income where you immediately start earning income or 3) a combination of both growth and income.

If you are in your twenties, thirties, or forties, the accumulation years, the rule of thumb is your investment portfolio should consist of mostly growth oriented investments that will appreciate over 10 to 30 years, rather than income investments. Percentage wise, your portfolio would consist of 60% growth and 40% income and savings. The reason is, you are young enough to use time to your advantage. You can wait for the growth investments to grow and to ride out any downturns in the stock or real estate market. If you are retired or close to it, your portfolio should weigh heavily in income and savings investments, where interest and income are paid to you regularly. Remember your financial objectives depend on your individual financial circumstances, so what is good for one person may not be for you. In Appendix C sample model portfolios are listed.

Spreading Your Risk— Diversification

Investment Pyramid

One of the first rules of successful investing and prudent portfolio management is diversification—spreading your risk. You should follow the old adage of never put all your eggs in one basket. It is virtually impossible to avoid all investment risk but through diversification you can minimize it.

The state of the economy plays a large role in determining what investment you should make. For example, if interest rates are rising, you should avoid the bond market, because bonds are considered interest sensitive investments and will lose their value if interest rates rise. If interest rates are declining, you will want to invest more money in the stock market, because stocks usually rise when interest rates fall.

It is impossible for you to predict what the economy will do in the future. You protect yourself by diversifying your investments to have a mixture of inflation hedge investments such as real estate, and growth stocks, which tend to do well. When the economy is in an inflationary state you invest in hedge type investments such as bonds.

The key is to have an investment strategy to minimize your portfolio risk. The crash of 1987 is a perfect example of why it is necessary to diversify your investment portfolio. On October 19, 1987, the Dow Jones Industrial Average lost 508 points in a single day. Many Wall Street analysts blamed computerized trading for causing the selling panic. Unfortunately no one can predict the volatility of the market. Many investors lost money that day, because they panicked and sold out too soon. Wise investors with a diversified portfolio and who knew they were investing for the long term had minimal risk and many took the opportunity to purchase additional stock while prices were low, so that today they have a handsome profit.

A portfolio building guideline is outlined in the investment pyramid **Figure 15-1**. The investment pyramid consists of 6 tiers. The bottom, **first tier**, is the base of the pyramid. The base is the foundation of your portfolio and includes your basic financial necessities and capital preservers such as your emergency savings in a money market mutual fund or another type of secured savings account, checking account, personal property —your home and life insurance.

The **second tier** consists of no risk investments such as CDs, treasury bills, tax-deferred annuities. You should place 25% of your portfolio in this area.

When you have accumulated funds and can afford to take some risk you should invest the next 25% (**third tier**) in low risk interest bearing accounts such as corporate bonds, municipal bonds, government securities and utility stocks.

In the **fourth tier**, 25% should be invested in blue chip growth stocks, high quality growth mutual funds, and real estate. These provide your portfolio with capital growth and a hedge against inflation.

In the **fifth tier**, 15% is invested in new and speculative growth stocks which also provide growth but because they are newly on the market they don't have a track record and are therefore a higher risk investment.

The **sixth and last tier** is only for the experienced investor who wants to speculate and take on a large amount of risk. The investments consist of commodities, options, and oil and gas tax shelters.

As you can see, the further up the investment pyramid you go there is an increasing risk of loss of your original money, but an increasing potential reward through appreciation. The key is not to jump tiers but to begin at the bottom and have each investment in place before moving on to the next level. Remember, this investment pyramid is only a guide. All investors are not created equal, and the investment strategy you should follow depends on your financial position and the amount of discretionary income you have available.

Socially Responsible Investing

Before you actually invest your hard earned money, there is a matter that you as a Black woman must consider: whether the investments you choose violate your moral or social beliefs. As we approach the twenty-first century we are finding that it isn't necessary to compromise our principles in order to make money. There are now many ethical investments that do not do business with South Africa, discriminate on the basis of sex or race, or support nuclear power.

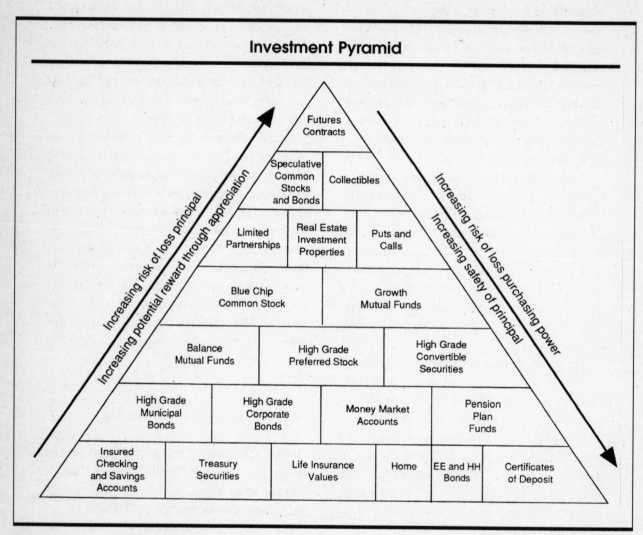

Figure 15-1 Investment Pyramid

Due to the acceptability of socially responsible investing there is a full range of investment options that are available to the socially conscious investor. They include stock and bond mutual funds and money market accounts. Skeptics of social investing previously claimed that it wasn't possible to make as much money with such a narrowly focused portfolio as it would if all stocks were taken into consideration. But recent performance ratings are now proving that investment portfolios that do not invest in South Africa related stocks perform as well or better than the market average. In fact, ethical investment portfolios were among the ones that held up during the October 1987 crash. Although the options and information on social investing have increased, it isn't always readily available and it is necessary for you to do your homework before investing.

Start first by contacting a socially responsible investment advisor. You can obtain a free list of advisors by contacting the Social Investment Forum, 711 Atlantic Ave., Boston, MA 02111, 617-451-3252. The Forum also publishes a quarterly newsletter, called the Forum, which provides additional information on social investing. The annual subscription price is $35.

CHAPTER 16

WALL STREET—INVESTING IN STOCKS

Investing in the stock market is still one of the best ways to make money. Many of you probably think of Wall Street as a jungle of fast talking and fast money, an area you could never really be a part of. Wrong—in fact chances are you already play a big part in Wall Street by having funds in your company's retirement plan.

As an investor, or potential investor, the stock market plays a vital role in your financial well-being. The market is the backbone of the American free enterprise system. It has over 45 million investors of whom half are women with an average household income of $33,000 and a portfolio worth $5,000. Investing in the market gives you the opportunity to share in the success of American business corporation.

Do not let the crash of 1987 scare you away. Based on past performance, stocks have out-performed corporate bonds and treasury bills over the last 40 years, in spite of the volatile up and down swings. The people who make money in the stock market, invest for the long term—2 or more years. If you want to make money in the market, you also must follow that philosophy.

The most common way to participate in the stock market is by investing in common and preferred stock. When you buy shares of a company's common stock, you become a part owner of that company. The number of shares you own relative to the total number of shares the company has sold (shares outstanding), determines the extent of your ownership. As a shareholder of a company you are entitled to the right to vote for company directors and major corporate policies. If the company prospers and grows, you have the right to share in the growth or capital appreciation of the stock, although there is no guarantee that the stock will increase in value. It could possibly decrease if the company is performing poorly. If the company makes a profit, the board of directors can vote to share by paying you, a common stockholder, dividends in proportion to the number of shares you own.

Preferred stock are equities that are senior to common stock. A preferred stockholder has priority in receiving his dividend before the common stockholders each year. The dividend is at a fixed rate and is usually higher than the common stock dividend. If it is a cumulative preferred stock, any dividends that had been previously omitted and accumulated must be paid in total, before common dividends are paid. For the preferred shareholder there are trade-offs. You do not have voting rights and your growth potential is very modest compared to that of the shareholder of common stock. Preferred stocks offer relative safety of income and are primarily for the investor seeking assured income. Both common and preferred stock are considered highly liquid investments, which can be sold at anytime.

There are three major categories of common stock: 1) blue chips, 2) growth and 3) income.

Blue chips are stocks considered to be high quality and of major well-established companies. They have long records of earnings growth and dividend payments in good times as well as bad. The stocks in the Dow Jones Industrial Average (DJIA) are considered blue chips. They are financially stable companies, for example IBM and Proctor and Gamble.

Blue chip stocks are a conservative investment that offers long-term growth with small dividend payments. Blue chips tend to be expensive because of their high quality and are usually out of reach for the beginning investor. If you have a financial portfolio consisting of ultra conservative investments such as CDs and treasury bills, blue chips are an excellent way for you to participate conservatively in the general growth of the economy.

Growth stocks are those of companies whose sales and earnings are growing at a higher rate than the general economy and faster than most stocks. These stocks serve as an inflation hedge type of investment for long term. The companies are usually very aggressive and research minded. They reinvest most of their earnings in the company to expand the operation and to generate improvements through research and development of new products. As a result, growth stocks pay very little dividend income.

The major reason for investing in growth stocks is to obtain substantial capital gains from the appreciation of the value of the stock as a result of the company's expansion. If the company consistently does well over a period of several years a small investment can grow with the company into a sizable amount.

The main problem with growth stocks is that the market price can be quite volatile. They often rise in price faster than other stocks but at the slightest hint of an earnings decrease the price can fall rapidly. New and small companies are particularly vulnerable when their earnings do not meet analyst and investors' expectations. Therefore, it is necessary to hold growth stocks for several years to obtain substantial gains.

On the investment pyramid, growth stocks fall on the fifth tier, where only a small percentage of your funds are placed unless you are an aggressive investor.

Income stocks are those of companies that pay out their earnings in the form of dividends to shareholders instead of reinvesting the money in the company. A good example of income stocks are utility companies.

Growth of the stock is usually very limited due to government regulations, but as earnings increase the dividend paid out to the investor can also increase.

When selecting income stocks, choose high quality companies that have a long record of increasing their dividends. If the dividend yield is much higher than other income stocks however, beware, for the company could be having financial difficulties. Paying out a large percentage of their earnings could jeopardize the company's future earning potential.

Income stocks are excellent for investors such as retired persons, pension plans and trust accounts because they offer high current income, some stability of principal and modest growth over the long term.

Wall Street

There are 2 classifications of publicly held stock: 1) listed and 2) unlisted (over-the-counter). If a stock is *listed* it trades on either the national or regional exchange. The New York Stock Exchange, (the big board) located on Wall Street in New York is the oldest and largest exchange. It lists and trades over 1,500 stocks. On the NYSE, stocks are traded by a two-way auction market supported by million dollar space-age computer systems to insure efficient and cost effective executions. The stock is worth only as much as somebody else is willing to pay for it. And the NYSE provides the place and

establishes the rules by which the trades are concluded.

Large exchanges include the American Stock Exchange, also located in New York, the Pacific Stock Exchange located in San Francisco, and the Midwest Stock Exchange in Chicago.

The Exchanges operate Monday through Friday, 9:30 A.M. to 4:00 P.M. (Eastern Standard Time). This is the only time you can buy and sell stock. Due to the recent changes in Europe there is current talk of a 24 hour exchange.

The second classification, *unlisted stocks*, also known as the "Over-the-Counter Market," has no meeting place. The stocks are traded by computers, through the National Association of Securities Dealers Automated Quotations (NASDAQ). Currently there are over 50,000 stocks trading in the over the counter market. The stocks range from high quality bank stocks to lower quality penny stocks. When a company is new it begins trading in the Over-the-Counter Market and as its assets increase and it becomes a more popular company it may apply to be listed on the NYSE. Some stocks such as Apple Computer have enough assets to be listed on the NYSE, but up until now have had no interest in moving to the big board.

DJIA—Dow Jows Industrial Average

The most popular stock index you have heard and read about is the Dow Jones Industrial Average (DJIA). It is a market index of 30 industrial companies that represent the major industries, such as oil, retail, chemical, and food. The stocks in the DJIA are often classified as blue chips. The purpose of the index is to reflect the overall consensus of the market. Many financial analysts claim the Standard and Poor 500 Index, another index consisting of 500 stocks, is a better indicator of the market than the DJIA. Both of these indexes are published daily in the business section of your newspaper.

Your Brokerage Account

In order to buy and sell stock you must establish a brokerage acount with a full service or a discount brokerage firm. (I will discuss the difference between a full service and a discount brokerage in chapter 24).

Once your account is open, your stockbroker transmits your bid, or the price you are willing to pay, to her firm's trader located on the trading floor of the exchange. The trader will then try to match your bid to the best offer (the lowest price for which someone is willing to sell the same stock). When a price between a buyer and seller is agreed on, then the transaction is concluded. A confirmation is then mailed to you stating the number of shares of stock you bought or sold, the price, commission, fee, the amount you owe or will receive if stocks sold, and the settlement date. You have 5 business days either to send in your money or, in the case of a sale, to turn in your stock certificate to receive your money. Once your account is open you can place buy and sell orders to your stockbroker by telephone.

Keys to Selecting Stock

The favorite adage on Wall Street is ''Buy low—Sell high.'' This is a feat that any Wall Street investor will tell you is hard to accomplish. Successful investing in common stocks is based on research, not rumors and hunches.

There are 2 techniques by which Wall Street professionals select stocks for their portfolio: *fundamental analysis* and *technical analysis*. It is essential that you learn the terminology of both techniques so that you are able to read and understand the research reports published by major brokerage house analysts.

Fundamental analysis, the most popular technique today, is based on investing in undervalued stocks—stocks of strong companies without debt problems that pay dividends and are lower priced than those of other companies in the similar industries. Fundamental analysis focuses on a company and its earnings as represented by its P/E (price earnings ratio) which is the calculation of share price divided by the company's earnings per share. For every listed stock this figure can be found in your newspaper stock table. Fundamental analysts look for stock with low P/E. During the past 30 years the P/E of stocks has averaged about 13. If a company's P/E is lower than the current market average it is said to be undervalued and a good buy. If it is much higher it is over valued and usually the stock of a fast growth company.

Fundamental analysts also look for companies whose shares are selling for less than the company is worth on paper. This figure is found by comparing the current stock price with its book value. The book value is calculated by taking the value of the company's assets, minus its liabilities and dividing the figure by the number of outstanding shares. If the current stock price is less than book value it is considered undervalued and a good takeover candidate.

Most of this research information on fundamental analysis can be found at your public library and through your stockbroker. Read the Standard and Poor Stock Guide, Standard and Poor—The Outlook, and the Value Line Investment Survey. These publications are full of research and statistics on many stocks.

Technical analysis is a method used by analysts who follow the theory that stocks perform based on past history. They select stocks by plotting charts and graphs of market trends. They look for any increases or decreases in volume of a stock on a given day and whether or not the stock price is fluctuating much more than usual.

This method of stock analysis is not recommended for the beginning investor. If you want more information on technical analysis discuss it with your stockbroker. Most brokerage houses have technical analysts who also publish reports.

The best method of selecting stocks for new investors is to first select an up-and-coming industry that you are interested in. Examples could be the food, retail, or automotive industries. Choose 2 or 3 companies within that industry and call or write the corporation for its annual report. Do not let the numbers intimidate you. If you're going to become a sophisticated investor, deciphering a company's financial report is essential. A company's annual report will supply a wealth of information on past and present earnings, new and current products it manufactures or distributes, and what if any new business plans it is working on.

Also listed in the annual report is an income statement. This will provide you with the current and previous year's sales volume, income, and any net profits or losses. By understanding what the numbers mean, you should be able to make an intelligent decision. The only problem is that it may not be the right decision. Selecting stock is an art not a science. And unfortunately the only way to learn is by sometimes losing money. So before you place a large chunk of your assets in the stock market, be sure to educate yourself and research each stock thoroughly.

Become a contrarian investor, which is one who does not run with the pack, but in-fact does the complete opposite. It will be hard not to conform and go with the crowd, but past research has shown that individuals who bought stock when everyone else was selling, and sold when everyone was buying have outperformed the overall market. Remember the crash of 1987, if you bought stock at that time and held it until now, your stock has probably appreciated 30–40%. Also read financial publications, such as the *Wall Street Journal*, *Barrons*, *Forbes*, and *Fortune* for general information on our company and its industry.

Reading a Stock Table

If you invest in individual stocks, you must understand how to read the stock tables in the financial pages of major newspapers. This information will help you track your stock's performance. **Figure 16-1** is an excerpt from a newspaper's alphabetical stock table. Let's assume you are interested in Walt Disney common stock.

Buying Stock on Margin

Buying stocks on margin is similar to buying stocks with your credit card. It allows you to buy stock by making a down payment and borrowing the remainder. These accounts are used by aggressive investors who want to leverage their investment and magnify their return. Such an account can be opened through a brokerage house or a commercial bank. For the beginning investor I do not recommend this method because of the risk of the market's moving against you. You can not only lose your down payment, but also may need to pay additional money to your broker to pay up the loss.

Building Your Stock Portfolio Without Commissions

One of the easiest and most affordable ways for black women to build their investment portfolio is through a program called the dividend reinvestment plan (DRIP), which is a low-cost (often no-cost) way of buying stocks for the long term. It may have an unfortunate acronym, but it's a good idea.

The plan allows you the shareholder to reinvest the cash dividends your stock earns into more shares of stock. You can also buy additional stock on a monthly or quarterly basis, often at a 2 to 5% discount to the current market price.

To participate in the plan, you must first become a shareholder by identifying a good company with strong earnings growth, a history of increasing dividend payments, and a dividend reinvestment plan, then purchasing 1 share of that company's stock from a discount broker. Take physical possession of the stock instead of having it held in "street name" at the brokerage firm. You are now a shareholder of the company. Write to the company and request an enrollment form for their DRIP plan. Aim to build your stock portfolio of 5 to 10 different companies using this method and purchase a regular amount of stock for each one every month or quarter. With the reinvestment of dividends and your additional purchases, you'll have a growing stock portfolio in no time. There are several newsletters and even a software program for people interested in this plan, I've listed some of them in the resource section.

Reading the Stock Market Pages

| 52 Weeks | | | | | Yld | | Vol | | | | Net |
Hi	Lo	Stock	Sym	Div	%	PE	100s	Hi	Lo	Close	Change
103 3/8	69 1/2	DigitalEqp	DEC	...	...	16	4064	83	81 7/8	83	+1
76 3/4	52 7/8	DillardStrs	DDS	.20	.3	16	450	71 3/4	70 3/4	71 3/4	−1/8
17 3/4	7 1/8	DimeSvgNY	DME	.60	7.6	...	436	8	7 7/8	7 7/8	−1/8
136 1/4	84	Disney	DIS	.58	.5	20	3737	110 7/8	109 1/4	110 1/2	+7/8
39	26	DivrsEngies	DEI	1.56	5.5	26	208	28 1/2	28 1/2	28 1/2	...
5 7/8	4 1/4	DivrsInd	DMC	...	...	19	17	4 1/2	4 3/8	4 3/8	...
48 5/8	41 7/8	DominRes	D	3.32	8.0	9	1937	42 1/8	41 3/8	41 3/4	−1/4

52—Week High/Low—the highest ($136.25) and lowest ($84.00) closing daily prices reported during the preceding 52-week period

Stock—company name (Walt Disney and Co.) and type of stock (common stock in this case: "pf" indicates preferred stock)

Div—the annual dividend paid for each share of stock during the preceding 52-week period (.58)

YLD—the return per share of stock, calculated by dividing the current market price (.58 ÷ 110.50 = .5%)

PE—the Price/Earnings ratio enables you to determine the company's latest 12-month earnings per share, calculated by dividing current market price by the figure given (110.50 ÷ 20 = $5.53)

Vol—trading volume, or sales, is printed in 100-share increments. In this case, 373,700 shares were traded during the day

High/Low—indicated the trading price range on that day ($110.875 high, $109.25 low)

Close—indicates the closing price that day ($110.50)

Net Change—the dollar amount by which the closing price per share advanced or declined from that of the previous trading day (in this case, a gain of $.87)

Figure 16-1—Reading the Stock Market Pages

CHAPTER 17

STOCK MUTUAL FUNDS

Investing in Stock Mutual funds

If you don't have a lot of money and still want to invest in the stock market, don't despair. You can still invest through mutual funds. A mutual fund is a portfolio of many stocks, bonds, or money market investments that are managed by the same company. When you invest in a mutual fund you buy shares of the fund's investment portfolio, making you a part owner along with other investors who have similar goals. For the novice investor with little capital, mutual funds are the safest and most convenient way to break into the stock and bond market.

There are 9 types of mutual funds with different investment objectives for you to choose: *growth stock, growth with income, income, corporate bonds, municipal bonds, balanced, government securities, global, and money market mutual funds*. Since we are discussing stock in this section we will only cover the growth stock, growth with income, income, and balanced mutual funds. The rest will be discussed later in the book.

A *growth stock fund* is a mutual fund, with a portfolio of aggressive or quality growth stocks. Its primary objective is long term capital appreciation. In this fund dividends are usually not paid to investors. Because this is an all stock fund, the value of the shares fluctuates with the stock market. You should not let the fluctuations scare you—your primary concern is long-term growth. If it does, you are in the wrong mutual fund.

Growth and income funds consist of stocks that pay dividends. Its objective is long-term capital growth with reasonable current income. The stocks are usually of well-established companies which have been paying a steady dividend. Due to the income factor, this fund tends not to be as volatile as "growth only" funds. A good example of a growth with income fund is a utility fund—a fund with a portfolio of utility stocks.

An *income fund's* primary objective is to provide a sizable and stable flow of investment income to its shareholders. The portfolio is generally made up of common stocks, preferred stocks and bonds, with high current yields being their investment goal.

Balanced funds are the most conservative of the stock mutual funds. Its portfolio consists of common stocks, high quality blue chip, preferred stock, and bonds. But its investment objective is security of principal, current income and capital appreciation over the long term. During stock market decline these funds experience less decline than other funds, but by the same token, during rising markets they generally lag behind.

Types of Mutual Funds

There are basically 2 types of mutual funds, open-end, and closed-end mutual funds. The most common and the better of the two is the open-end.

Open-end mutual funds have an unfixed number of shares available to investors. The number of shares continues to change as investors purchase new and redeem (sell) shares. When purchasing you buy directly from the fund and if you want to sell, the fund must buy them back from you.

The price to buy or sell shares is based on the daily computed net asset value (NAV) of the day. The NAV is the total value of all securities held by the fund divided by the number of outstanding shares, a figure computed daily at the close of market.

A *closed-end* mutual fund, which recently has become popular, is similar in many respects to an open-end fund except it issues a fixed number of shares. Because it is sold by stock brokers and trades on the stock exchange or the over the counter market, the price of the share is set by the supply and demand of the market place not the net asset value. Some of the most popular closed-end

funds selling today are funds that specialize in stocks of a particular country such as Korea, Taiwan, Spain, Australia, or Italy.

When a closed-end fund is initially offered to the public it sells at a premium and it isn't a good time for you to invest.

After the initial offering period, the fund frequently sells at a discount from their net asset value, sometimes as much as 10%. This is the time to invest, because you get more for your money. There is usually a sales charge commission to buy or sell closed-end funds.

Load and No-Load Mutual Funds

Open-end mutual funds are sold on either a load or a no-load basis. A load is a commission charged to you, the investor, by the fund for executing the transaction. There is also a management fee of usually ½ of 1% per year of the fund's assets in addition to the sales load.

There are four classifications of load mutual funds: *high-load, low-load, 12b-1, and no-load funds*. High-load mutual funds charge you between 4 and 9.3% commission on your investment. Front-end means there is an up front sales commission charge so that if you invest $10,000 with an up front commission of 6%, $600 will go toward the commission and your actual investment is $9,400. If you sell a back-end load fund, the sales commission is deducted from your earnings or losses. Many of the back-end loads become no-load funds after your money is invested for 5 or more years in the fund. If you withdraw your money during the first 5 years you will be charged a yearly declining sales commission.

Low-load mutual funds charge 3% or less when you either invest or withdraw your money. The sales commission is not paid to stockbrokers and financial planners. The mutual fund companies use the money for advertising and other expenses.

A 12b-1 fund is a no-load mutual fund that charges an extra 1% fee per year for marketing costs. 100% of your money is invested and the 1% fee is deducted from your earnings. There has been a lot of controversy regarding whether or not it is really necessary for these funds to charge this extra 1%. Before you invest in this type of fund, compare the performance record with no-load funds that do not charge a 12b-1 fee.

A no-load mutual fund does not charge you a sales commission to invest or withdraw your money.

Load vs. No-Load Funds

Now that you know the difference between load and no-load funds, your next question is which one should you invest in? There isn't a right or wrong answer. It mainly depends on you. Each of the funds has benefits and drawbacks. Load funds are sold by sales representatives and financial planners who advise you on the type of fund that will meet your investment objective. If you are really new at investing or do not have the time to

research mutual funds thoroughly, then load mutual funds are for you. However, you should never let another person tell you what to do with your money. Always have some ideas of the type of investment you want.

No-load funds are not sold through sales representatives but directly from the company. So you eliminate the middleman. In return you pay no sales commission and have full responsibility of researching, buying, and selling the fund.

No-load funds are excellent investments for the individual who wants to take complete control of her finances. Most no-load funds have a smaller minimum to open than load funds. In terms of performance, there is no evidence that shows a loaded fund performs better than a no-load. In fact, they are very equal. My recommendation for you is to do your own research and invest in no-load funds. After all, the purpose of your reading this book is to become financially independent and have complete control and knowledge of how to invest your money without having to pay exorbitant sales commissions which can take a huge chunk of your investment dollars.

Benefits of Investing in Mutual Funds

For the small investor, investing in mutual funds offers 4 major benefits over buying individual stocks or bonds. First, by pooling your money with other investors you are able to invest in a large diversified portfolio of stocks or bonds. Your money is spread among many different securities within the fund. Because of this diversification, if one of the stocks within the fund plummets in value due to problems in the company, the rest of the stocks in the fund will cushion your investment, lowering your overall risk.

Second, a mutual fund offers experienced professional management to select and monitor the securities in the fund. They decide when to buy and sell sparing you the work and research of following each individual stock.

Third, mutual funds offer convenience and liquidity for investors. Most funds can be purchased through the mail and for as little as $25 to open. You can withdraw part or all of your money anytime you wish by a phone call or a letter.

The fourth benefit is the investment options and exchange privileges. If you invest in a family of funds, your investment options are limitless. You can invest in stock, bonds, international companies, precious metals, and money market instruments. If for any reason your investment objective changes, most funds will allow you to exchange into another fund within the family for a nominal charge or fee.

Choosing a Stock Mutual Fund

Choosing a stock mutual fund isn't as difficult as you might think. Several sources of information on mutual funds are readily available. The most commonly used is the prospectus prepared by the mutual fund company. It gives information on the fund's investment objective, how to purchase, and redeem shares; the minimum initial and periodic investment; the composition of the fund's portfolio; names of the managers and directors of the fund; the fund's financial statement and the performance of the fund over the last 5 to 10 years.

It is wise for the novice investor to select mutual fund families. A family offers a number of individual funds with different investments and objectives. They may include stocks, bonds, money markets, international stocks and bonds, specialty and precious metals. By investing in a family, you have a wide variety of investment options to choose from. Your goal is to make sure the fund's investment objective meets with your own objectives. Look at the past performance of the fund. Compare it to other funds with the same objectives. Do not look just at the last year which may not be indicative of the real performance of the fund. Research the last 5 years. The key you want to measure is how the fund performed during both a bull (up) and bear (down) market.

Look over the securities in the portfolio, and ask yourself a few questions. Are they companies you would invest in outside of the mutual fund? And do they meet your moral and ethical objectives? If the answer to these questions is no, don't invest. Instead research for another fund that would meet your approval. Is it a load on no-load fund? If it is a load fund compare its sales charge with similar funds. It's best to find the lowest or no-load fund with a good performance record. Invest in a fund that offers you convenient purchase, sell and exchange privileges. And the information regarding your investment should be readily available by contacting a mutual fund representative through a toll free number.

A very important factor in choosing a mutual fund is the overall economic climate. Are interest rates moving up and stock prices moving down? If so, maybe you should first invest in a money market fund and then later switch to a stock fund. Read the financial pages and magazines daily. Soon you will have some idea where the economy is going and at which time you can make your investment move.

The Best Way to Invest in Mutual Funds

Dollar Cost Averaging

The best technique for investing long term in a mutual fund is dollar cost averaging, which means investing the same amount of money into the same mutual fund at regular intervals. The advantage is that you buy more shares when the price is lower and fewer shares when the price is higher. The average cost per share of the investment is less than the average market price per share over the period you are investing, enabling you to capitalize on price fluctuations of the mutual fund. See **Figure 17-1**.

It does take discipline to invest this way each month. If that's a problem for you, most mutual funds now offer bank draft au-

thorizations. They will automatically deduct the same amount of money from your bank account each month. This way you are assured of investing in the dollar cost averaging technique without having to write a check every month.

This method of investing does not mean you will not lose money. It does mean that your losses will be less if you started investing at a bad time and you will have gains if you start investing at a good time. If you sell your mutual fund shares when the market price of the stock is below the average cost of the share you purchased, you will have a loss. If you sell when the shares are above your average cost, you then have a profit. You must remember that mutual funds are long term investments and regardless of the daily price fluctuations you should continue to invest. The time you should consider selling your mutual fund is when you have reached your financial goal or if your fund is consistently performing poorly compared to similar type funds. And even then don't be too hasty to sell. Research thoroughly before making your final decision.

Reading the Mutual Fund Tables

The mutual fund table located in your newspaper is different from the stock table. Mutual fund tables list whether it is a no-load or load fund, and the daily changes in the price of the fund. If it is a mutual fund family it will list all the fund names and quotes. See **Figure 17-2** for a mutual fund listing.

Dollar Cost Averaging: How Regular Monthly Investments Cost Less

Investment Amount	Shares Purchased	Share Price
200	20	10
200	8	25
200	5	40
200	13	15
200	10	20
$1,000	56	$110

Average Cost
Per Share:

$$\frac{\text{Total Investment Amount}}{\text{Shares Purchased}}$$

$$(1,000 \div 56 = \$17.86)$$

Average price
Per Share:

$$\frac{\text{Total Price Per Share}}{\text{Number of Purchases}}$$

$$(110 \div 5 = \$22)$$

The average price per share was $22—but your average **cost** was $17.86. With regular monthly investments instead of one lump sum purchase, you paid $4.14 less per share over time!

Figure 17-1 Dollar Cost Averaging

Reading the Mutual Fund Chart

	Sell	Buy	Chg
20th Century:			
Ballny	11.25	NL	–0.4
Gift	8.72	NL	–.02
Growth	16.27	NL	–0.7
Heriny	7.14	NL	–.04
LTBnd	90.12	NL	–.17
Select	33.84	NL	–.15

The first column is the abbreviated fund's name. Several funds listed under a single heading indicate a family of funds. In this example the name is 20th Century Family of Funds and the fund's name is the Growth Fund.

The second column is the Sell or Net Asset Value (NAV) per share as of the close of the preceding business day. This is the amount per share you would receive if you sold your shares (less the deferred sales charge if any). This fund's sell price is 16.27.

The third column is the buy or offering price— the price you would pay if you purchased shares. The buy price is the NAV plus any sales charges. If there are no sales charges, a NL for no-load appears in this column. Example—this fund has NL so it is a no-load Fund.

The fourth column shows the change, if any, in net asset value from the preceding quotation —the change over the most recent one-day trading period. This fund for example, lost 7 cents per share.

Figure 17-2 Reading the Mutual Fund Chart

■ **NOTES**

CHAPTER 18

BONDS AND BOND MUTUAL FUNDS

Investing in Bonds and Bond Mutual Funds

If your investment objective is primarily to obtain income with guaranteed return of principal instead of growth then you should consider investing in bonds. A bond represents a loan to the issuer (IOU). You, the investor, lend a sum of money to a borrower for a specific period of time. The amount you lend is called the principal and is paid back to you on the maturity date, which can range from 60 days to 30 years later. The longer the maturity the higher the amount of interest that is paid to you. In the meantime, the borrower agrees to pay you interest every 6 months for the use of your money. The interest rate, which is also called the coupon rate, is fixed; it will not change for the life of the bond. For example, if you invest $10,000 in a U.S. government bond that pays a 10% coupon rate, which will mature in 5 years, you will receive $500 every 6 months until the bond matures, a total of $5,000. At maturity you will also receive your $10,000 original principal.

Bonds look like the perfect risk free investment, but unfortunately, they aren't—if you decide to sell your bond before the maturity date, your initial $10,000 may be worth more or less money. The price of bonds fluctuates with interest rates and inflation. If interest rates and inflation increase, the value of your bonds will decrease causing you to lose money if you sell before maturity. But the opposite can also occur. If interest rates and inflation decrease, the value of your bond will increase, providing you with a profit if sold early.

Another risk associated with bonds is called credit risk. Not all bonds are created equal and there is a possibility that due to default your bond will not repay your original principal at maturity. Therefore, it is important that you understand the rating system of bonds and the types of bonds that have the greatest risk.

How Bonds Are Rated

Bonds are rated for safety and financial strength by 2 independent rating firms: *Moody's Investor Service* and *Standard & Poor*. Standard & Poor ratings range from AAA, the highest, to D, the lowest, and

Moody's ratings range from AAA to C. The higher the rating the lower the coupon rate you receive because of the added extra security of the insurer. Conservative and inexperienced investors should only buy bonds rated A and above, and stay away from those rated BB, BA, or below; which are speculative and higher in risk.

The following types of bonds are listed in order of their increasing exposure to risk of default:

U.S. Government Bonds—These bonds are backed by the full faith and credit of the U.S. government and have no credit risk.

Municipal Bonds—These bonds are issued by state, cities, and municipalities which are tax exempt authorities. There has been one major exception of default—Washington Power Supply System bond (WPPSS)—but rarely are there defaults.

High Grade Corporate Bonds—These are issued by corporations and secured by the corporation's property.

Junk Bonds—(High Yield)—These bonds are used primarily for acquisitions of other corporations: Default of these bonds is common, and therefore they are normally sold in mutual funds.

Call Date

Another feature of bonds you should understand before investing is the call date. The insurer of the bond can request you to turn in your bond before the maturity date. Usually this is because overall interest rates have fallen and they no longer want to pay you a coupon rate that exceeds the current market rate. Many bonds do have call protection. Check with your stockbroker or financial planner before you invest.

Types of Bonds

There are numerous types of bonds to invest in. Which is best for you will depend on your goals, income, and the amount of risk you are willing to take. The following is a summary of bonds to aid you in making a decision.

Federal Government Bonds

The federal government offers several bonds; a few include treasury bills, treasury notes, treasury bonds and series EE bonds. Since the government has the highest credit rating of any borrower (although this is questionable) its bonds are considered the safest, and therefore, pay the lowest.

Treasury Bills (T-Bills)

Treasury bills mature in 3, 6, or 12 months. The minimum initial purchase is $10,000 with $5,000 increments thereafter. These bills are issued at a discount and pay the face amount at maturity. Your return is the difference you receive between the cost and face amount of the bill. Interest on T-Bills is exempt only from state and local taxes.

There is liquidity in T-Bills because they can be sold before maturity.

Treasury Notes

Treasury notes have maturities from 1 to 10 years. The interest is paid semi-annually at a fixed rate. If the maturity is 4 or more years, they are available in minimum amounts of $1,000. If maturity is shorter the minimum is $5,000. These bonds cannot be called and the interest is exempt from state and local taxes. The yield on treasury notes is higher than T-Bills, but you run a risk of your treasury note losing value if interest rates rise.

Treasury Bonds

Treasury bonds mature from 10 to 30 years or longer. They are also insured and backed by the government. Because of their longer maturities, the yields are higher. They also are non-callable and the interest is exempt from state and local taxes.

Series EE Bonds

Series EE bonds pay no current interest; instead they are issued at a discount and the full face value is paid on the maturity date. Interest is exempt from state and local income taxes and federal taxes are exempt until you cash them in. They are sold in face-value denominations of $50 to $10,000 and in purchase price from $25 to $5,000. In order to earn the minimum market based interest rate of 6%, you must hold the bonds for 5 years. Series EE bonds can be purchased through most banks and many employers offer employees an automatic payroll deduction plan to purchase them. Because of their low initial cost, they are an excellent way to save for your child's education.

Municipal Bonds

Municipal bonds are one of the last true tax havens since the Tax Reform Act of 1986. These are bonds issued by cities and states. The interest on most municipal bonds is exempt from federal income tax. If the bond is issued by the state of your residence, the interest is state tax free as well.

Municipal bonds sell in $5,000 denominations or they can be purchased through a mutual fund for a minimum of $1,000. The yields are less than treasuries and corporate bonds because of their tax-exempt status.

Most municipal bonds are non-callable for at least 10 years. These are excellent investments for women in a high tax bracket who want tax-free income. These bonds are rated by Standard & Poor and Moody's. Quality of the bond is important to reduce the possibility of default resulting in the loss of your principal. To evaluate whether you should invest in municipal bonds; **Figure 18-1** compares what another investment with a taxable yield would have to yield to be equivalent to the tax-free yield of municipal bonds.

Tax-Free vs. Taxable Income

Taxable Income (1,000's)	Combine State and Federal Tax		Tax-Free Yields 6.00% 6.50% 7.00% 7.50% 8.00%				
Single Return	Joint Return	Rate (Rounded)*	Equivalent Taxable Yields				
$20.87-26.38	$41.75-52.76	33.8%	9.06%	9.82%	10.57%	11.33%	12.08%
$26.38-47.05	$52.76-78.40	34.7%	9.19%	9.95%	10.72%	11.49%	12.25%
$47.05-97.62†	$78.40-162.77†	39.2	9.87	10.69%	11.51%	12.34%	13.16%
over $97.62††	over $162.77††	34.7%	9.19%	9.95%	10.72%	11.49%	12.25%

* Rates for 1990 federal and state taxable incomes based on figures available at press time.
† The top figure for the 1990 maximum federal tax bracket of 33% will increase by $11,480 for each dependent claimed in the return.
†† Based on the Tax Reform Act of 1986, federal income taxes decrease to 28% for these income brackets.

Figure 18-1 Tax-Free vs. Taxable Income

Find your tax bracket—the amount after all your exemptions and deductions—and read across to the taxable yield you need to obtain to match the tax-free yield. If you are single with taxable income of $25,000, you are in the 33.8% tax bracket—(federal and state taxes), and a tax-free yield of 7.00% is equivalent to a taxable yield of 10.57%. If you are unable to invest your money in a taxable investment yielding 10.57% or more, than you should consider investing in tax-free municipal bonds.

Corporate Bonds

Corporate bonds are those issued by corporations. Some of the major issuers are electric, gas and telephone utility companies, banks and railroads. These bonds are sold in minimum amounts of $1,000. Maturities range from 1 to 30 years or longer. They yield about 2 percentage points higher than U.S. government bonds because of the higher risk factor. The interest income on corporate bonds is subject to federal, state, and local taxes, and paid is every 6 months to the bond holder.

Many bonds can be called away early for a price slightly higher than the maturity value. Like other bonds, corporate bonds can be sold before the maturity date at the current market value, which can be higher or lower than the original face amount. This will depend on what the rate of interest and inflation is at the time the bonds are sold. If safety is an important factor, stick with corporate bonds rated AAA or AA by Standard & Poor and Moody's.

Junk Bonds

Junk Bonds are low quality corporate bonds issued to finance takeovers, and to assist financially troubled corporations and new firms that need to raise money. These bonds are rated BBB or less and pay a much higher yield because of the credit risk. There is no guarantee that the issuer will pay interest and principal upon maturity.

Junk bonds have maturity dates of 5 to 30 years and can be purchased for as low as several hundred dollars per bond to $1,000 in a mutual fund. These bonds are for the sophisticated investor who is willing to assume a high degree of risk. The safest junk bonds are rated B or BB and are issued by companies with healthier financial conditions than the ratings suggest.

Zero Coupon Bonds

Zero coupon bonds are those issued at a deep discount from face value that pays zero interest until maturity. They are similar to the series EE bonds, discussed earlier. For example, you can pay $250 for a $1,000 bond maturing in the year 2000 and receive the full face value of $1,000 at maturity.

Zero coupon bonds are issued by corporations, municipalities and the U.S. government, which is the largest issuer. Brokerage houses have various names for them; some you have probably heard of are Tigers, Cats, and Strips. The advantages of zero coupon bonds is that you know exactly how much money you will receive when the bond matures. So it gives you an opportunity to plan for something specific like a college education or retirement.

The annual yield for zero coupon bonds is about 1 percentage point higher than non-zero treasury bonds of the same maturity. The longer the maturity of the zero coupon bond the higher the yield.

Zero coupon bonds have 2 distinct disadvantages. The first is, even though you do not receive the interest until maturity, the Internal Revenue Service requires you to pay taxes each year on the interest you have earned. You can usually avoid this tax bill by buying the bonds in your child's name (but see page 57 for details on income shifting). Or if the money is designated for your retirement you can buy the bonds in your Individual Retirement Account or Self-Employed Pension Plan.

The second disadvantage is that the bond values tend to fluctuate more than other types of bonds because of the way they are discounted. If you need to sell a bond before its maturity date and interest rates have changed, you are much more likely to take a loss. Which is why these bonds should be purchased only as a long-term investment— 10 or more years.

The safest zero coupon bonds are those issued by the U.S. Treasury. Before investing ask your broker or banker about all fees and commissions on zero coupons and the bond's yield to maturity.

Bond Mutual Funds

Bond mutual funds are similar to stock mutual funds except their portfolios consist of bonds instead of stock. Of the many bond funds available, you can select from corporate, tax-free municipal, government, foreign, and junk bonds.

These funds provide wide diversifications reducing the risk of bond investing. They are professionally managed, eliminating the need for you to correctly time the purchases and sale of each bond. Bond funds like stock funds are liquid. You can buy and sell any time. The minimum to invest is usually $1,000. Most provide monthly or quarterly interest income depending upon the fund.

Many bond funds are part of a family of funds, allowing you to switch from stock funds to bond funds without a fee. Some bond funds are no-loads and others are loads with sale charges ranging from 4 to 8½%.

Bond mutual funds are highly recommended for the investor with limited funds. You should select a bond mutual fund the same way you select a stock fund. Look at the total return of the fund, which includes the yield and any change in the share value. Compare at least 5 to 10 years of performance with other comparable bond funds.

The yield on bond funds is not fixed and guaranteed, so the amount you receive monthly or quarterly can change. Also the value of your shares can increase or decrease depending upon inflation and interest rates.

Ginnie Maes

Another investment for those seeking regular income is the Ginnie Mae certificate. It is one of the highest yielding government securities available. Ginnie Maes are mortgage backed securities, guaranteed by the Government National Mortgage Association, a U.S. government agency. These are available through your stockbroker or financial planner for a minimum investment of $25,000. The interest and repayment of the principal are guaranteed by the U.S. government and are usually paid out monthly as the mortgages are being paid off. In the early 1980s, Ginnie Mae Mutual Funds became available, allowing the small investor to participate. The minimum to invest in these funds is $1,000 to $2,000. The funds provide high yields and diversifications. Like the $25,000 Ginnie Mae certificate, interest income is generally paid monthly, and many of the funds allow you to reinvest your monthly interest and principal payment.

The main drawback of Ginnie Maes is that you are buying a mortgage and you cannot predict when the principal on the Ginnie Mae mortgages will be repaid. Your monthly income and principal fluctuates month to month. Some mortgage holders pay off their mortgages early, others later depending on the current mortgage rate.

The maturity on Ginnie Maes usually lasts for 12 years, but there is no guaran-

tee. There is a possibility your Ginnie Mae certificate could be paid off early forcing you to seek an alternative place for your money.

■ NOTES

_____

_____

_____

_____

_____

_____

_____

_____

_____

_____

_____

_____

_____

_____

CHAPTER 19

GOLD, SILVER, AND OTHER PRECIOUS METALS

When you have built a base and a stable investment portflio, you can consider investing in gold, silver, and other previous metals such as platinum. As you recall in figure 15-1 of the investment pyramid, a small percentage of your portfolio, 10%, is dedicated to gold and other precious metals.

For your portfolio of traditional securities, start at 1% and build to a maximum 10%. Gold and silver offer protection when inflation is high or during political unrest and economic uncertainty.

There are a number of ways to invest in precious metals: Through mutual funds, mining stocks, bullion, bars, coins and commodity futures. Because they specialize in research and knowledge of mining and production companies, mutual funds are the best method for investing in precious metals. Mutual funds free you from the worry of transport and safekeeping and offer distinct advantages over direct ownership of bullion, bars, coins, and futures. Liquidity is one such major advantage. Some funds pay dividends and they generally are not as speculative as futures contracts in the commodity markets.

Bullion and bars should not be considered unless you plan to purchase a large amount and leave it in the bank. The reason for this is that bullion and bars are not immediately liquid. Every time they are bought or sold they must be atuhenticated or tested for purity (assayed). Bullion, bars, and coins are non-income producing assets. You do not earn money while they are in the bank or in your possession. You must hold them indefinitely until there is price appreciation of the metals from high inflation.

Another popular way to invest is through coins, which are very liquid and do not require to be assayed upon resale. Easily stored, they can be kept in a safe-deposit box.

Commodity futures offer a highly leveraged, extremely speculative way to participate in precious metals. Unless you are a professional speculator willing to take high risk stay away from this investment.

■ NOTES

CHAPTER 20

GLOBAL OPPORTUNITIES— INTERNATIONAL INVESTING

The next decade will bring about significant changes in the financial marketplace. The United States is no longer the only land of financial opportunities. With money now flowing freely from one market to another by satellites and computers, global opportunities to make money abound. it is important that black women understand the international financial marketplace as well as the domestic financial marketplace. You should participate by placing at least 10%–15% of your assets in the international markets.

Almost half of the world's investment value is outside the United States. Showing clear evidence by their high volume of investments in the United States, foreign investors know all about the U.S. markets. They are your competition in the battle for financial survival.

Diversification of your investment portfolio is another reason why you want to invest internationally. By diversifying, you reduce your overall risk and increase your potential for profitable gains. In the 1970s the best stock market opportunity was out-

side of the United States. And in 1985 this pattern was repeated due to changes in the U.S. dollar value and fluctuations in world interest rates. An investor during that time made more money in the international major stock markets than here at home. 1985 proved to every investor that it was necessary to invest with an international perspective and that watching world stock trends opens up a world of financial opportunities.

International investments do have their pitfalls and risks. Foreign stocks are valued in currencies other than the dollar, so whenever the foreign currency value changes, the value of the stock changes. When the value of the dollar goes up or down, foreign stock may lose or gain in value. So you have 2 ways to make money. One is through the appreciated value of the foreign investment and the other is the rise in the value of foreign currency versus the dollar.

Another pitfall, is that choosing a foreign security is more complicated than picking a U.S. stock. The research about a foreign company is made difficult for an American investor to evaluate by the use of different accounting methods abroad and the U.S. requirement of more disclosure than foreign companies. Also, it is difficult to evaluate the effectiveness of management whose performance standards differ from those in the U.S.

Other problems include high commission cost, political risk, foreign taxes, liquidity problems and restrictions that other countries impose on foreign investors. In spite of these problems, foreign investments should still be a part of your investment portfolio.

Two methods of investing in foreign securities that will minimize your risk:

The first for the more sophisticated investor who wants to purchase individual stock, is through American Depository Receipts (ADRs). These are foreign stocks that are traded in the United States. They can be bought or sold through your U.S. broker without any complications. The stock trades in U.S. dollars and dividends are paid in U.S. dollars. An ADR is a receipt issued by an American bank certifying that the bank holds an equivalent number of foreign shares. Two of the largest insurers of ADRs are Morgan Guaranty Bank and Citibank in New York.

The ADRs that trade on the U.S. market tend to be blue chip international firms that have well known products in the U.S. such as Sony from Japan, Jaguar from England, L'Oreal, Perrier, Club Med, and Peugot from France. Not all foreign stocks are traded in the U.S. in the form of ADRs, so there are some limitations to choosing stock in foreign markets. There are 500 ADRs available in the United States. Obtain as much information as you can on an ADR before you invest. Investing in ADRs is not recommended for the novice investor.

The second and best method to invest in international securities is through mutual funds. With as little as $1,000 you can become an international investor. The professional management and diversification of a mutual fund relieves you of the research burden. Of the 3 types of foreign mutual funds, two are open-end and one is a close-end fund. The 2 former are called global funds and international funds, the first consisting of a portfolio of U.S. and foreign securities and the second is an international fund consisting entirely of foreign securities.

The closed-end fund is a mutual fund consisting of stock in one country, such as Japan or Italy, that trades on the U.S. exchange. Their shares are priced just as any ordinary stock in the open markets. The technique for picking the right fund is similar to buying ADRs. You must research the market before investing.

In 1986, single country funds became popular investments and as a result, the share prices were bid up to a premium, selling for a price that was greater than their real value. Do not pay a premium for a closed-end country fund. The key rule is to buy in a low priced, out-of-favor market where your potential for gain is much higher.

Foreign investing is still a relatively new area for the U.S. and many brokers and financial planners are not familiar with foreign stocks and ADRs. To obtain information, try the public library and read *Barrons*, *The Wall Street Journal*, *The New York Times*, and the *Los Angeles Times*.

Investments in South Africa and Other Emerging Markets

South Africa is undergoing sweeping political and economic change. As the country continues to move toward a free market economy, the opportunities for financial growth for the aggressive investor who is willing to take some risk can be substantial.

South Africa is viewed as one of the leading contenders among emerging markets. The Johannesburg stock market is the tenth largest financial market in the world.

During Apartheid, Africans and African Americans were unable to participate in the financial wealth of this country. Well, that has now changed. You can contribute to the economic development of the African continent by investing in the Calvert New Africa fund, a mutual fund that invests monies exclusively in Africa and is managed by an African-American financial firm. The fund will invest in companies trading on the African stock exchanges and also act as venture capitalist by providing money to small businesses and black entrepreneurs. But you must use caution and only invest money you can afford to lose. There is still much political uncertainty within the African continent and it is difficult to gauge the future of their financial markets.

When investing in any emerging market, whether it is South Africa or South America, I recommend investing through a mutual fund and not individual stocks. Read the mutual fund prospectus carefully and talk to your financial advisor. If it sounds like it's too good to be true, it probably is—avoid it.

119

CHAPTER 21

BENEFITS OF JOINING AN INVESTMENT CLUB

Joining an investment club is an excellent way for a black woman to acquire confidence in managing money. It provides a good introduction into the mysteries of the financial world when you have limited funds.

An investment club consists of a group of investors who get together and pool their cash resources, each making a monthly contribution of $10 to $25, which is used to purchase stocks.

Various types of clubs range from women only, men only, married couples, senior citizens, or young people. It is important that all members become actively involved. Each member in the club is responsible for generating stock ideas that are investment possibilities. Everyone researches the stocks and makes reports and recommendations to the others. The group then decides to buy or sell a stock through either a full service or a discount broker. If the group is new to investing it is recommended that it works with a full service broker in the beginning. The goal of the club is to develop a diverse long term portfolio of growth stocks in different industries.

Most clubs are affiliated with NAIC, the *National Association of Investors Corporation*, a non-profit organization designed to assist groups interested in starting an investment club. The organization publishes a monthly magazine called *Better Investing* which provides information on investment and stock analysis. The NAIC's philosophy is that investment clubs invest in long-term growth industries and reinvest all dividends and capital gains from the sale of any stock held in the portfolio instead of paying it out to the members. This will compound the value of the portfolio.

If you are interested in starting an investment club, select people with a variety of interests and with compatible investment goals. Even though there can be a social side to the club, investing is serious business and the goal of the club is to learn and earn. After participating in a club for a while, most members are able to start their individual portfolio based on the education and information they received as club members.

For more information on NAIC, contact The National Association of Investor Corporation, write NAIC, 1515 East 11 Mile Road, Royal Oak, MI, 48067.

Key Steps to Start and Manage an Investment Club

African-American women throughout the country are coming together in the spirit of sisterhood to learn how to make money and have fun at the same time. They are starting investment clubs. They are pooling their resources together to reach their goals of financial security. The Washington Women's Investment Club and the Atlanta Black Women Attorney's club are 2 successful examples. Starting with a $500 capital base, each amassed within 5 years investment portfolios worth over $50,000. What was their secret? They managed the club like a small business whose sole purpose is to make money. They did so by sticking to the following guidelines:

1. Select members wisely. The members are the key components of a successful club. Ideally, you should select people with whom you have something in common such as friends, church members, associates from sororities or other organizations, neighbors, and co-workers. Ten to 20 people is a manageable number for the club. Anything larger than that may invite personality conflicts which lessen the likelihood of reaching a consensus. You also want people who will be active participants and attend the meetings. The purpose of the club is to learn. If a large percentage of the members are people who only send in money, the club won't last.

2. Decide on the amount to invest, the meet ing day, time, and location. The monthly club investment should range from $20 to $50 per member. Meetings are commonly held in a home, library, or office conference room.

3. Select a name for the club and obtain a tax-ID number from the IRS. You will need this number to open a brokerage account with a licensed discount brokerage firm.

4. Elect club officers. Choose a core group of 4 to 5 people to keep things organized. The president usually leads the meetings and assigns hostesses and researchers. The vice-president arranges for invited speakers or other types of educational programs. The secretary takes minutes at each meeting. The treasurer reports the buy and sell orders to the club's broker and maintains all financial records.

5. Form a legal partnership. The partnership does not pay federal income tax, but each individual partner is liable for taxes on her share of the club's gain. Even if all club income from dividends, interest, and capital gains (profits from sales) is reinvested, income tax is still owed on the money. At year's end, the treasurer should give each member a report of her individual share of the club's income, gains and losses. This information is reported on each member's 1040 tax form. The club should also hire a CPA to review the club's end-of-year statements.

6. Establish club bylaws. Include laws on emergency withdrawals, when a member resigns, or how a new person joins. Think of every conceivable problem and solution and spell it out in the bylaws.

7. The first month of the year (January), plan out the year's monthly meetings and determine a list of stocks or investments to research. Each member should give a stock report at every meeting, as well as a monthly review of a different industry, such as retail, food, health, etc. The report should consist of the sales and earnings of the company and an analysis of the stock price history (its highs and lows). If the member thinks her stock should be included in the club's portfolio she should present her case at the meeting.

8. Set goals. A good goal is to try to double the dollar value of the club's investment portfolio every 5 years while attaining an average annual growth rate of 15%. While in the learning phase, the portfolio may lose money or make only a small gain, so be prepared.

Aim toward owning 100 shares in a company, even if you buy only a little at a time. Select a downside and upside percentage. In other words, if a stock drops 15 to 20%, the club agrees to sell the stock and take the loss, or if the stock is up 50%, the club agrees to take the profit. Once you've made your decision don't look back. There are plenty of stock opportunities out there.

9. During the beginning stages you may want to hire a financial advisor or stockbroker for assistance. A full-service broker will make stock and investment recommendations for a higher fee than a discount broker. A discount broker will not give financial advice and charges less for stock purchases. An investment advisor will provide advice and may charge by the hour or a percent of the amount he or she manages plus a discount brokerage commission. Once your club is established, you may only want to meet with an advisor or broker annually.

10. Research all investments before you buy. Consult the following periodicals that are available in most public libraries:

• Value Line Investment Survey
• Standard & Poor's Stock Reports
• Morningstar Mutual Fund Newsletter
• Company Annual Reports (contact the shareholder's department at the company's headquarters)

11. Avoid "paralysis of the analysis" —go ahead and make the investment. Don't spend months or maybe even years researching a stock but never actually making the investment. I've seen more investment clubs fall apart because the group was never able to make a decision on which stock to buy. Find a stock, bite the bullet and buy it. If you make a mistake, it's no big deal. Learning how to make money takes patience.

12. Join the National Association of Investment Clubs listed above. They will supply you with information to help jump start your club.

■ **NOTES**

CHAPTER 22

WEALTH ACCUMULATION THROUGH REAL ESTATE

Achieving financial independence through real estate investing is not a new concept in the African-American community. Many black Americans who have achieved the American dream of financial security have made their wealth by either starting their own business or investing in real estate.

Real estate investing will continue as a major wealth builder and a much sought after commodity. This increase in demand will cause substantial appreciation in real estate prices and will provide black women who invest in real estate with an opportunity to make money.

Every year in the month of September and October, *Fortune* and *Forbes* business magazines publish a list of the billionaires and 400 richest people in America. Most of the individuals on the list made it because their real estate investments were a major portion of their investment portfolio.

Foreign investors, particularly Asians and Europeans are well aware of the value of real estate. They consider real estate prices in the United States bargains compared to prices in their own country. They are stead-ily purchasing properties throughout the country, many of them located in the inner cities of New York, Los Angeles and Chicago. These properties range from expensive high rise office buildings to single family homes in the black, Hispanic and Asian communities.

For black women seeking financial independence, it is essential that you own not only your home but other real estate as well. There are 2 reasons for owning real estate. First, there is a tax advantage, and second, land is scarcer and the hurdles created by the government to construct more buildings on the land that is available has increased ten-fold. At the same time, the human population is increasing in leaps and bounds resulting in more people chasing a limited supply of real estate thus causing significant price increases.

In the beginning, the real estate game may seem strange. The terms and the concepts may be difficult to grasp but like anything else, the first step is always the hardest. With preparation you will soon realize that success does not require extraordinary knowledge or talent. It does take a willingness to learn the real estate market. Do your homework and persevere. Your determination will yield the most success. Ignore the doomsayers, there will always be someone to tell you it won't work. Trust and act on your instincts.

Becoming a successful real estate investor also entails building successful relationships with bankers, real estate brokers and attorneys in your community. They can supply you with a wealth of information and lead you to profitable real estate deals. You will need to keep abreast of the real estate market. Real estate reacts immediately to changes in the economy. If you are well versed on the subject, you can react quickly to the changes which can yield you enormous real estate profits.

Buying Your First Home

Home ownership in America is an integral part of the American dream and the single largest investment you will probably make in your lifetime. Unfortunately many African Americans have been led to believe that a first home is hopelessly out of reach to them. Many are continuing to pay out large sums of money for rent, preventing them from building equity in property to increase their net worth.

It is true that incomes in many areas are not keeping pace with inflation and rising home prices. And the banks, savings and loans and other lending institutions have also tightened their mortgage qualification standards requiring a much larger down payment of 10-20% of the purchase price. But all is not lost. There are people today buying their first home with the use of creative financing. The money is out there. You have to find it.

The future for first time home buyers is also beginning to look brighter. As of this writing there are several bills before Congress, expected to be in place by late 1995-1996 that will improve your chances of buying a home.

For first time home buyers the bills would allow withdrawal of funds from IRAs and 401(k) employee account without penalties.

The legislation will also increase the Federal Housing Administration's (FHA) mortgage insurance limit of $101,250, to 95% of the median sales price of a home in a given area. This will enable people in high cost areas such as California and New York where home prices far exceed the current limit to obtain FHA financing. The act will lower the FHA's down payment requirement from 5% to 3% for first time home buyers. It will also insure adjustable-rate mortgages that are competitive with private lending institutions.

Before you start looking at homes it is essential that you calculate how much you can afford to pay for a house. **See figure 22.1.** The cost of a home not only entails your loan mortgage payment but also closing cost, property taxes and maintenance fees. Be sure to include them in your affordability calculations.

The House You Can Afford

For a House That Costs:	With a Down Payment of:	Your Monthly Payment Is:			
		8%	10%	12%	14%
$80,000	$ 8,000	$528	$632	$741	$853
	16,000	470	562	658	758
$120,000	12,000	793	948	1,111	1,280
	24,000	704	842	987	1,138
$200,000	20,000	1,321	1,580	1,851	2,133
	40,000	1,174	1,404	1,646	1,896

This chart is based on a 30 year, fixed rate mortgage.

Figure 22-1 The House You Can Afford

Mortgage shopping

When applying for a mortgage loan you should be aware of certain guidelines used by lending institutions:

- The price of the home should not exceed 2½ times your annual gross income.
- Your housing payments, long-term debts and major fixed expenses should not exceed 36% of your income. If you make a down payment of less than 20% it should not exceed 33%.
- The total annual payments for your mortgage, homeowners insurance and property taxes should not exceed 28% of your gross income.

Your first priority for buying a home will be to lower your long term debt and credit debt to enable you to qualify for a mortgage.

Types and Terms

Selecting the right mortgage has become just as important as selecting the right piece of property. Before choosing you must shop around and compare interest rates, mortgage maturities, points, closing costs and the required down payment. Many local newspapers publish the rates of several lending institutions in your area or you can contact a real estate or mortgage broker who has the current rates.

The 2 types of mortgages are, 1) fixed rate mortgages and adjustable rate mortgages (ARM). With a fixed rate mortgage the interest you pay on the loan never changes throughout the life of the loan. With the adjustable rate mortgage (also known as variable rate mortgage) the interest rate fluctuates depending upon leading economic indicators such as the one year T-bill yield or the "cost of funds" index from the federal home loan bank board.

Both types have pluses and minuses. If interest rates are low, the fixed rate mortgage is the best. It provides you with a predictable monthly mortgage payment and has none of the surprise increased monthly payments of the adjustable rate. On the other hand, the fixed rate is usually 1 to 3 points higher than an ARM, which is the premium you pay for certainty. Therefore in periods of tight money and high interest rates, the first time home buyer will find it much easier to qualify for the ARM than the fixed rate.

If you decide on or can qualify only for an ARM, ask lots of questions before signing on the dotted line. Questions to ask are: When does the initial interest rate on the ARM adjust? It is usually after 6 months. What index is the loan tied to? What is the ceiling on the percentage the interest rate can be raised annually (CAP) and the life of the loan? Typically it is 2 percentage points a year and a total of 5 points over the life

of the loan. And last, is there a prepayment penalty for paying off the loan ahead of time? This you would do if you were to refinance for a fixed mortgage rate.

Once you've decided on the type of loan you want, your next decision is whether to take a 15 or 30 year conventional mortgage. Recently the 15 year mortgage has become popular and has 2 major advantages. 1) The rate on the loan could be a ¼ to 1 percentage point lower than a 30 year loan. 2) Your total interest payments are cut approximately in half enabling you to build up equity in your home quicker. The disadvantage of the 15 year loan is the higher mortgage payment you will have to make. On a $75,000 loan at an interest rate of 10.75% for a 30 year mortgage, your monthly payment is $700.11. On the same amount at a fixed rate of 10.5% for a 15 year mortgage you would pay $829.05 monthly. For many people this is too much of an increase to handle.

Due to the constant changes of interest rates and economic indexes, lending institutions change mortgages to reflect the market place. Two recently developed mortgage variations which you may want to consider are the biweekly mortgage and the convertible ARM. With a biweekly mortgage you make a payment every 2 weeks cutting your total interest cost dramatically. The convertible ARM begins as an adjustable rate mortgage but lets you switch to a fixed rate between the second and fifth year of the loan. There may be fees for converting to these new loans.

As mentioned earlier, your mortgage payment is not the only expense you will incur when purchasing your home. Other fees to investigate (called "upfront costs") can range from a hundred to several thousand dollars. They include the loan application fee, the loan processing fee and points. One point is equivalent to 1% of the loan amount. Most lenders charge 2 to 3 points. Many lending institutions will lower your points if you agree to pay a higher mortgage rate. This is okay if you cannot afford to pay the upfront cost but can pay the higher mortgage payment. However, beware of no-points mortgages. With this mortgage you pay for the points over the life of the loan thereby increasing the size of your mortgage loan and payment. This is an expensive cost. You save money by paying the cost upfront.

Other fees include title search, survey, homeowner's insurance, attorney fees, pro-rated property taxes and private mortgage insurance (PMI). The last is required by many lenders if you make a down payment of less than 20%.

Other Creative Ways to Buy Your Home

When all else fails, there are other creative alternatives to help you buy your first home. Sweat equity is still a viable means of buying a home. If you have the time and aren't afraid of getting your hands dirty it can be well worth it. For your best choice, look for

a nice neighborhood where a fixer-upper has become such an eye sore that it is priced below the market. Fixing it up increases its value—and so does its good location, so that you will more than likely make a profit if eventually you decide to sell.

Lease Option

An attractive alternative to renting is a lease option agreement between the renter and owner of the property. The renter leases the property paying a monthly rent, with an option to purchase the property from the owner at a later date. In certain agreements, part of the rent goes toward the eventual down payment. Lease option agreements are flexible and can be written to give you ample time to buy and save for the down payment. Your attorney should look over the lease option agreement.

Equity sharing

Equity sharing is great for the person who can afford a mortgage payment but is unable to furnish the down payment. Under this agreement an investor provides the down payment in exchange for a share of the profit when the buyer sells the property. Equity sharing contracts are written by an attorney and can be written to suit the needs of both partners. Your parents, business associates and real estate clubs can be excellent partners for equity sharing. Your real estate agent or mortgage broker can tell you of companies specializing in equity sharing.

Seller Financing

Seller financing is a viable alternative if you are having trouble qualifying for a mortgage. In this case the seller finances the deal accepting monthly payments from you at rates that are near or above the current mortgage interest rate.

State or Local Housing Agency

Your state or local housing agency may provide financial aid for first time home buyers. There is usually a limitation on your annual income and the price of the house in order for you to qualify for the subsidy, which can come in the form of a low down payment or a mortgage with a below market interest rate.

VA/FHA Loans

If you are a member of the armed services, a veteran or the spouse of a deceased veteran you may qualify for a mortgage that is backed by the Veterans Administration. There are 30 year fixed rate loans that require nothing down. You can obtain a VA loan for a maximum of $144,000. The interest rate is generally below that of conventional loans. In order to obtain this loan you need a certificate verifying you or your spouse's military service. Call your local VA office to obtain a certificate and a list of VA loan institutions.

The FHA loan is an insured loan available to anyone who applies. The required down payment ranges from 3-5% and you can obtain a mortgage of $67,500 or $101,250 in areas that are considered high cost by the FHA. The interest rates on FHA loans are at or below the market rate. The mortgages are available in fixed and adjustable rate loans.

HUD/Probate Houses

Another excellent source for first time home buyers is buying one of the many homes that are offered through the Department of Housing and Urban Development. These are homes that have been acquired by the department after the owner had defaulted on the FHA mortgage. They are offered at prices that are 10-40% below market value. You can find out about these homes through your real estate agent or the local HUD office.

A probate house is one being sold as part of an estate. The heirs of an estate are usually eager to sell the assets and distribute the money quickly and therefore may accept a lower price. You can learn about probate or estate sales by checking with your county courthouse records.

As you can see, home buying is not out of reach. With a little legwork and some creative financing, you can join the ranks of many Americans who own their own home.

Investment Real Estate

Tax Reform Changes:

The Tax Reform Act of 1986 had a detrimental effect on the tax benefits of real estate. The new law affected 3 areas in particular:

- **Depreciation**—Under the old law investors were allowed to depreciate residential real estate over 19 years. The new law requires you to depreciate residential property bought after 1986 over 27.5 years and commercial property over 31.5 years, which means you can deduct only a small percentage of the purchase price as a paper loss on your tax return each year.
- **Capital Gains Tax**—The new law eliminated the favorable tax treatment for property held long term, thus requiring you to pay taxes on the gain at your regular tax rate, meaning a larger portion of your gain will be paid out in taxes.
- **Tax Losses**—There is now a limitation on the amount of tax loss you can claim on your rental property. The deduction you are allowed depends on how actively you manage the property and the size of your income. The new law allows you to deduct up to $25,000 of the property's losses against your salary and other income as long as you own at least 10% of the property and actively engaged in the management of the property. Also your

adjusted gross income just be less than $100,000.

The Tax Reform Act has basically closed the loopholes that many wealthy investors were using to avoid paying taxes. The properties heavily hurt were the large office buildings and apartment complexes. As a result, there has been a reduction in the construction of these types of properties. This reduction will cause an increase in prices of existing properties due to short supply and increased demand. The government now wants you to invest in real estate for growth and income rather than for a tax shelter.

Benefits of Real Estate

In spite of Tax Reform 1986, there are still many benefits of including real estate in your investment portfolio. The 4 major ones are 1) Tax advantage through depreciation and interest deductions. 2) Capital appreciation—real estate is an excellent inflation hedge, because when inflation increases real estate prices generally rise.

Consider yourself fortunate if you bought your home in the 1960s or 1970s because your home is worth much more today due to the inflation of the 1980s. 3) Income generator—real estate can provide a great source of income generated from renting and leasing of the property. And last 4) Leverage—you can buy and own real estate with only a partial amount (sometimes less than 10%) of the purchase price.

There is 1 disadvantage of real estate

and that is liquidity. You can't sell real estate as quickly as you can stocks or bonds. It may take months to receive an offer at the price you want. Therefore when you invest in real estate you should plan on holding on to the property for at least 3-5 years.

Types of Real Estate

There are various ways of investing in real estate. The most common and direct method is ''hands on real estate.'' It requires the highest amount of cash outlay and much of your time to manage. With this type of investment you have the most control over your property and pay the lowest amount of fees and commission.

Properties included in this category are single family homes, multiple dwellings such as a duplex, office buildings and raw land.

The second method of investing is ''hands off real estate.'' It is an indirect method of investing. You do not personally manage the property. Two types in this category are real estate limited partnerships and real estate investment trusts (REIT). The required cash outlay for this type of investment can vary from $1,000 to $5,000.

The method you choose will depend on the time, effort and money you are willing to commit. If you are a new investor and want to manage your own property you should consider residential rental real estate, particularly properties with more than one rental unit such as a duplex or larger. The more tenants you have, the fewer chances of one vacancy having an adverse effect on your monthly rental income.

You should purchase real estate that is close to home, enabling you to check on the property frequently. Location of the property is a major factor for your profit potential. Look for a well maintained neighborhood close to schools, shopping and transportation. Look for fixer-uppers in a desirable neighborhood. Do not buy the most expensive home in a run down neighborhood hoping that the area will go through a gentrification. Your investment may not pay off.

Investing in rental property unfortunately does not guarantee you positive cash flow. With high mortgage payments and property taxes, many properties have negative cash flow. At one time this was great, when you were allowed to deduct your losses from your income taxes. Since Tax Reform 1986, the rules have changed. Negative cash flow deductions are now limited and therefore it is unprofitable for you to invest in this type of property.

If you are an investor with limited time and money, real estate limited partnerships and real estate investment trusts (REIT) are a viable alternative. A limited partnership is composed of 1) a general partner who provides the professional expertise and management skills and who is willing to assume unlimited liability and 2) the investor, who is considered a limited partner. You provide the money, have limited liability and enjoy the benefits of investing in major real estate projects that you ordinarily would not be able to afford.

Two types of real estate limited partnerships are available through financial advisors: *registered* and *private placements*. Both types buy and develop apartments, office buildings, shopping centers, business parks and mini-warehouses. A registered limited partnership is offered to the public. It must be registered with the Securities and Exchange Commission (SEC) whose main function is not to approve or disapprove of the offering but to make sure that "full disclosure" of all information relative to the offering is made available to the investor. This information is made available through a prospectus, which you should read before you invest your money.

Register limited partnerships are large offerings of $50 million or more. The money is diversified in several properties. You can invest as little as $2,500 or $5,000 in an individual account or $2,000 in an Individual Retirement Account-IRA.

When selecting a registered limited partnership, look for one with a long term track record in both up and down markets. *The Stranger Register*, a publication available in brokerage offices and some libraries rates registered limited partnerships.

In a private placement partnership the general partner is allowed to have a maximum of 35 limited partners. The partners pool between $10,000 and $100,000 from each investor to buy or develop 1 property. The money you invest can be paid in annual installments over 5 or more years. Since the SEC does not require the general partner to register the partnership, it must be thoroughly scrutinized because the risks may be high.

Before tax reform, private partnerships were used by the wealthy to obtain tax breaks. They were able to deduct twice the amount they invested off of their income taxes. Now with Tax Reform 1986 the amount that can be deducted is substantially lower.

The biggest disadvantage of investing in limited partnerships is the illiquidity. Once your money is invested you must wait several years, until the partnership sells the property, to get back your money. Some program sponsors will buy back your units but usually at a substantial loss to you.

If the illiquidity factor is of concern you can buy shares of a real estate investment trust (REIT).

A REIT pools money from investors and invests in properties just like a limited partnership. The difference is that you can sell and buy shares anytime just like a stock. REITs must pay their shareholders 95% of the rental and interest income they receive. The yields on REITs can range from 6-12% annually. Since REITs trade like stocks, their share prices rise and fall with the stock market. Plan to keep your shares for at least 3 to 5 years. At that time the plan is most likely to sell some of the properties and pay out the profits to the shareholders.

Five Steps to Successful Real Estate Investments

Investing in real estate is very extensive and should be included in your program to obtain financial independence.

The 5 steps you need to invest successfully in real estate are:

- **Perseverance**—there is still opportunity to make money in real estate.

- **Ignore the negative people** who tell you it can't be done or it won't work.
- **Do your homework**—know all you can about the real estate market and the property you are interested in buying.
- **Build relationships** with your banker, broker, and attorney in your community. They can help you with your real estate deals.
- **Act now**—the longer you wait to invest in real estate, the further away you are from reaching your goal of financial independence.

■ NOTES

_____

_____

_____

_____

_____

_____

_____

_____

_____

_____

PART 4

PUTTING IT ALL TOGETHER

CHAPTER 23

AFRICAN-AMERICAN WOMEN, MONEY, AND DIVORCE

Divorce is an emotional and financial upheaval in any woman's life, but African-American women are much more vulnerable and many feel insecure when handling their finances during this turbulent time. Unless you are schooled in the family finances and have an attorney working on your behalf, the probability of you obtaining a decent financial settlement is low. So *sisters, listen up* if you don't want to run the risk of falling into poverty after your divorce.

When your marriage is falling apart money is the last issue you want to discuss, but let me remind you this is *the most important issue*. There are horror stories after horror stories, too many for me to tell you in this book, about African-American women getting burnt financially during their divorces. It's a trying time for both parties, and there's a lot of pent-up anger and resentment. How many times have we heard of one spouse taking all the money out of the joint savings or checking account without the other's knowledge?

Rachel Edwards, mother of 3 young children and an administrative assistant at an insurance company, learned her lesson the hard way. When she initiated divorce precedings against Stan, her husband of 10 years who is a physician, he withdrew the entire $25,000 balance from their joint savings account and charged up to $10,000 on their joint credit cards. According to Emma Pendergrass, a black matrimonial attorney who works with many African-American women, this happens frequently during a divorce. Before seeing an attorney you should close all joint credit card accounts and destroy the cards for which you may be liable. You also need to close and equitably divide all liquid assets as joint savings and checking accounts, investment securities, or any other valuables that can be converted into cash. Once this is completed, both parties are then on equal financial playing fields. That's the proper time to consult an attorney.

Protecting Yourself Financially

A couple's financial records are a vital commodity in a divorce. The person who takes care of the finances and keeps track of the financial records is in the power seat and has a tremendous advantage.

You need to know each asset that you acquired during your marriage, where it's located, and what its value is. All assets are part of a marital estate, which will be divided by the divorce judge. You'll also need proof of assets, such as the latest bank statements as well as statements for the last 5 years. You should also gather old tax returns and check registers, especially if you think your spouse may have been siphoning off money and hiding it in anticipation of a divorce.

Having a good attorney to work on your behalf is essential because he or she will also examine assets that are not in both your names and decipher whether they are personal, marital, or a little bit of both. During a divorce most couples focus on savings, checking, and investment accounts, and their home. But there are other assets to consider. One in particular is your pension or individual retirement account which may be worth thousands of dollars. If the account grew while you were married you'll need to turn over part of the money to the other spouse and vice versa. Vacation days, season tickets, and college degrees also fall in the category of marital assets. Any accrued vacation time or paid leave may be considered

a special asset that can be converted into cash and become part of the divorce settlement. If you have season tickets to sports or cultural events you need to assess their replacement value. The partner who doesn't get the tickets should be compensated.

In years past, I've heard of several women who were the sole wage earner and full-time mom while their husbands were in medical or law school. Once they graduated and began earning 6 figures, the men claimed their wives were no longer desirable and asked for a divorce.

Spouses who have worked full time while the other partner pursued a medical, legal, or graduate degree may now have a little more protection. These days, a college or professional degree acquired during the marriage is considered a joint asset. Your attorney should calculate the worth of such an asset using the present value of all monies invested to acquire that degree. He or she should use the "what if this money had been invested in an interest bearing account" scenario, to determine how much it would be worth now. In the calculation you need to include tuition, books, parking, lab fees, food, etc. If the degree has enabled your spouse to start a professional practice or open a business, the value of this degree may be considered a divorce asset.

When You Make More Money Than He Does

Statistics show that more black women than black men are seeking advanced degrees. With this increase in education comes higher incomes for African-American women. Therefore, the likelihood of a black woman making more money than her man is high. If this is the case in a marital breakup, black women need to know that they may get stuck with an alimony bill.

Samantha Davis, a controller with a Fortune 500 company earned an annual salary of $90,000. Her husband, Eric, was laid off 2 years ago from the local utility company. After several unsuccessful attempts to start his own business he became emotionally and verbally abusive toward Samantha and their 2 children. After a thorough analysis of her alternatives, Samantha decided to file for divorce. Eric immediately lashed out at her by taking money out of their joint accounts. He had also secretly photocopied all of their financial records and tax returns and took them to his attorney who helped him obtain a $4,000 monthly alimony payment. Because he was unemployed and she made a lot of money, he was able to snag a large amount. It didn't matter that she paid the house note and the expenses that went along with it as well as private school tuition for the 2 children.

When the divorce laws changed in 1980 to provide for fair and equal distribution of marital assets, it was thought to be a break-through for women. But because of today's economy and particularly because of high unemployment rates, black men are not afraid to ask for alimony. And you don't necessarily have to make a large income. Even if you're making $30,000 a year, he's going to go for it if he's not working.

The way around this problem is to aim for a property distribution, not alimony. That way, you make 1 lump-sum payment and it's settled.

Financially on Track after the Divorce

Once the dust has settled, it's time to look to the future. Know that within yourself *you will* be able to adjust and survive financially. If at all possible, seek the advice of a financial consultant who can give you guidance and help you to get back on track.

Setting New Financial Goals

Begin to look at your divorce as an opportunity to wipe the slate clean and make positive changes in your life. You can first begin by setting new goals for yourself. Take time to really focus on what *you want* to do with your life. Write out a wish list of all the things you want your life to include. Be open-minded and dream big. When you've completed your list, start thinking about what it would actually take to turn some of your wishes into reality. Would you like to go back to school to complete or obtain an advanced degree? Then call your local community college and make an appointment with a counselor. You may qualify for an all-expense-paid scholarship that will actually allow you to quit your job and go to school full time. But you won't ever know unless you make that call. I have said several times in my public talks that knowledge is power. The people who are successful seek out knowledge and as a result are privy to the wealth in this country. We too, as African-American women can obtain some of this same information. But first we have to know what it is we want. When we are focused, it's amazing what we can accomplish.

Recreating Your New Monthly Budget

More than likely, your financial position has changed since your divorce. Your income and expenses may have either decreased or increased. Regardless of which one, you need to create a new monthly budget. Go back to chapter 6, "Cash Management," and complete the Money Management 101 worksheet. If you have payments that you make several times a year, add them up, divide by 12, and enter the monthly average in the appropriate space.

Does your total monthly income equal your total monthly expenses? In other words, does the cash that comes in equal the cash that's going out? If you have money left over at the end of the month, that's good news, but if it's the opposite then we have a problem, and you'll need to either increase

your income or decrease your expenses. If it looks next to impossible to cut back on your expenses, then you seriously have to consider a way to bring in more money. Maybe this is the time to turn your jewelry-making hobby into a part-time business. Get creative and use your imagination to find a solution to bring in extra money.

Calculate Your New Net Worth

When you were married, you completed your net-worth statement as a couple. Once you have agreed to a divorce settlement, you need to repeat the procedure to determine your new net worth. Use **Worksheet 4-1** in chapter 4, "Current Financial Standing." Look at the last line of your net-worth statement. Do your liabilities exceed your assets? If your answer is yes, it's probably your credit card debt that's causing the problem. You need to work on eliminating it. I'll show you how in the next section. Unless there is a change in your financial status, I encourage you to compute your net worth once each year, preferably at the same time each year for comparative purposes.

Debt Management

After your divorce is an excellent time to implement a plan to get rid of your debt. Start by listing all your debts and the amount owed on the "Get out of Debt FAST" worksheet located in the appendix. Once this is completed look at your list and decide which bill must be paid first. Factors you want to consider are the date on the bill and the amount of the interest rate. The oldest and highest interest rate bill should be paid off first.

If bills have gone unpaid because of the divorce, I suggest you contact your creditors by letter. You may have been avoiding or evading them but you cannot continue to do this. Your letter should:

- Outline the reason for the unpaid bill— you may wish to state that you just went through a divorce, and that you are now in a position to pay off your debt.
- Inform them how you will pay them and the amount you will send in each month.
- Let them know the date by which you will begin payments—you should include a check with your letter to show good faith.

Most creditors will work with you and your payment plan as long as you keep them informed of any financial problems you may be having. They would rather you send in a small payment than no payment at all. If the creditors approve the plan, be sure to stick to it because they usually only give you one chance.

Insurance

Review your health, dental, life, and disability insurance policies. Make sure you and your children have adequate coverage. You may also need to change the beneficiaries on your current policies.

Investments

Right after your divorce is not the time to make major investment decisions. It's better to put your money into a money market fund or interest bearing account until things in your life are a little more organized. Also make sure you have 3 months of living expenses set aside in a savings account.

When you feel more comfortable with your new life and your future plans are relatively clear, you can slowly move your money into investments where it can work harder for you.

Plan Your Estate

As a newly divorced woman, don't assume you don't have enough property to "plan your estate." If you wrote down anything in the assets column of your net-worth statement, or if you have children, you do need to plan your estate, starting with a will. As your assets increase, you'll want to consider a trust.

Jumping the Broom— Prenuptial Agreements

African-American working women who have accumulated assets such as real estate, investment portfolios, and large pension plans may want to consider a prenuptial agreement before they enter into marriage. With the advent of equitable distribution laws, a rise in the divorce rate, and a high number of second marriages, you can use a prenuptial agreement as a marriage contract to spell out the consequences of a breakup or death, similar to the way partners in business would sign a contract.

While this may be a touchy subject for most couples, for many already established women it makes economic sense. The nature of marital property continues to expand to include professional degrees and pension funds. In other words, if you have a pension fund worth $100,000 at the time of your marriage, and you continue to add money to the fund during your marriage, the fund is then considered joint property and is subject to be divided in the event of a divorce. Your spouse may receive 50% of the total amount even though you had already accumulated $100,000 in the fund before you were married. The only way this may be avoided is with a prenuptial agreement that would exclude the assets from division.

What Is a Prenuptial Agreement?

It's a marital contract whose purpose is to spell out what to do with the property you hold individually or jointly with your spouse in the event of a divorce or death. If it is written before the marriage, it is called a prenuptial, or antenuptial agreement. It is also possible, but not common, to write an agreement after the marriage. That is called a postnuptial agreement.

The prenuptial agreement basically covers the following 4 issues:

- **Assets and Liabilities.** Both parties must list the assets they each own and how much they are worth. You must decide which assets will continue to be owned individually and which ones will become marital property. You must also state how much debt and what type of debt you each owe. A decision must also be made about gifts and inheritances. Will they be shared or kept separate?
- **Divorce.** If you decide to end the marriage, you can state whether or not alimony will be paid, how much, and the terms—lump sum or monthly. You will also outline how you will split assets brought to the marriage and purchased during the marriage with joint funds.
- **Estate Plan.** In the event of the death of either spouse, you can designate who gets what. Will your assets go to children from a previous marriage or to children you may have in the future?
- **Retribution.** If one spouse limits his or her career success and loses pension benefits because of family responsibilities, or if one spouse brings in more liabilities than the other, you can state in the agreement how each spouse will be compensated.

Why You May Want a Prenuptial Agreement

While the main reason for prenuptial agreements is to protect the spouse with the most assets, agreements have become almost mandatory for second marriages, where the husband and wife want to keep some finances separate so that children from a first marriage will inherit their property.

Here are some other reasons you may want to consider a prenuptial agreement:

- You have a lot more money than the man you are marrying, and you want to keep control of your own money.
- You are remarrying, and you want to protect your existing money.
- You live in a community property state, and you don't want to give up half the assets you accumulate in the future.
- You live in an equitable distribution state, and you don't know how the court might divide up your assets should the marriage end, so you want to establish your own terms.
- You have a family business, and you don't want it to end up with his family.
- You are a partner in a business, and your partners don't want the control of the business to pass outside of the company.
- You or your spouse is an entrepreneur, and you want to separate the business from other marital property and make provisions for the business's succession and survival.

Hire a Professional

If you want your agreement to be airtight you must be very careful in drafting it or it will not hold up in court. Judges have the authority to toss out an agreement that doesn't measure up to their standard. This is definitely not a do-it-yourself project. There are too many variables that a professional would know to look out for that you could miss. You should hire a professional to help you get it right. It is also imperative that you and your spouse have separate counsel. If you ever end up in court, the spouse who signed the agreement without legal representation can claim that unfair advantage was taken by the lawyer who drew up the contract.

In order for the prenuptial agreement to hold up in court, it must meet the following conditions:

1. Full disclosure of all financial information. The fastest way to invalidate the agreement is to try to hide some of your assets. If the marriage doesn't work out, and your spouse discovers assets you didn't disclose in the agreement, the whole contract could be thrown out.

2. It must be fair. If the court thinks the agreement was significantly unfair to one spouse the whole thing can be thrown out. The contract has to represent a reasonable arrangement taking into account your individual assets, ages, earning abilities, and business sense. Some states require you to also take into consideration the health of both parties, your prior standard of living, and the welfare of your children, both past and future.

3. Each spouse must enter into the agreement without pressure. The agreement will not hold up in court if the judge finds it was made and signed under emotional stress or threat that the marriage would not happen unless it was signed. For protection, lawyers are now videotaping the signing of the contract to show that both parties were fully aware of what they were doing and acted on their own free will. So, don't wait until the day of the wedding to have your spouse sign the agreement.

Going Through the Steps

While a prenuptial agreement isn't for everyone, going through the steps is. Money is the number one reason why marriages end in divorce. Every couple should talk about their finances before the wedding day. It helps to lay the foundation for a trusting and successful marriage. You should both draw up a list of what you're each bringing to the marriage in the way of assets and debts. If you find your future spouse is reluctant to discuss his finances, take heed, he may be trying to hide something, or he may use money as a source of power and control which could lead to trouble in the marriage later on. Don't allow your emotions to get in the way of making judgements with your finances.

CHAPTER 24

ESTATE PLANNING
NOT JUST FOR THE RICH

Estate planning is an essential part of your financial plan. It allows you to provide financial security for your family after your death. You can decide how your property is to be divided among your heirs and who the legal guardians of your children should be, not the state.

Many women die **intestate**—without a will. Many feel they don't own enough assets to justify a will. Everyone has some property they must dispose of. You probably own a lot more than you think.

Dying without a will

If you die intestate—without a will, your state has special laws called the ''laws of intestacy'' that control how your property [real estate, checking, savings account, stocks and bonds, and personal assets] are divided up. If you have young children, the state will also determine who their guardians will be.

The size of your taxable estate is based on the current market value of the property held in your name, your share of property you own jointly with someone else, the death benefit of your life insurance policy and assets you have in a revocable living trust. If the combination of these assets exceeds $600,000, your heirs will have to pay federal estate taxes. When you combine your house, life insurance, retirement plan at work, car and other personal belongings it isn't hard to reach $600,000.

The first dollar over $600,000 is taxed at 37%, anything over 3 million is taxed at 55%. Depending upon the size of your estate, the government can take a huge chunk of your assets from your heirs which is why it is necessary for you to have an estate plan. With proper planning you can reduce or eliminate taxes leaving more money to your family.

The first step in putting together your estate plan is to make an inventory of the assets that form your estate and determine their value. (**Worksheet 23–1**) List everything you own, including such items as real estate, stocks and bonds, equity in a business, jewelry, art, furniture, cars, and your checking and savings account. Also list money you may have in an IRA, company pension and profit sharing plan, and the value of all life insurance policies.

Your first priority is to make sure that your survivors will have enough money to cover their basic needs. An emergency cash reserve fund can take care of the living expenses for a few months in case your life insurance death benefits are delayed. You need to carry enough life insurance to cover your family's living expenses, estate taxes, and the cost of probate. Probate (to be discussed later) can take 6 months to 2 years and cost 10% of your estate.

Before you draw up a will, you need to select someone to act as your executor. This person is responsible for paying your taxes and debts, getting your assets appraised and distributing your property to your heirs and beneficiaries. If your estate is less than $600,000, you can ask your spouse, another relative or your adult child. Your estate can then save having to pay an executor fee which can range from $4,000 to $20,000 depending upon the size of your estate.

If you are a parent you need to ask someone to become the guardian of any minor children [those under 18 in most states], in case you and your spouse die at the same time. Seek an individual who shares similar philosophies in raising your children and has the time to take care of yours. It is not always recommended to select the grandparents because of their age. They might not live long enough to complete the job. It is also a good idea to select alternate guardians in case of an unforeseen problem.

If you are the parent of a disabled child who will need a guardian for life, you will need a different type of estate plan. Any money left to him or her could make them ineligible for Medicaid, which pays medical bills for the needy. Instead you can leave extra money to another child who agrees to take care of the disabled child. Or you could invest in an annuity that will provide regular payments to them.

There is also a special trust called the "*family sprinkle*" that provides benefits for family members without affecting the Medicaid eligibility. Discuss this with your family attorney.

The guardians you select will be responsible for the children as well as their money and property. You should select someone who knows how to handle both. If you are unable to find someone who meets both qualifications, you can select 2 guardians, one to take care of the children, the other to manage their money, possibly a financial institution.

Your Will

Regardless of your age or the amount of assets you have, you need a will. The purpose of a will is to make sure that your property goes to those you want it to go to, rather than to the people your state chooses under the intestacy laws.

Estimating the Size of Your Estate

Description	Wife	Amount of Worth Husband	Combined Total of Estate
Life Insurance Ⓐ	$_____	$_____	$_____
Residence Equity Value Ⓑ	$_____	$_____	$_____
Savings Accounts	$_____	$_____	$_____
Business Ownership	$_____	$_____	$_____
Pension and Profit	$_____	$_____	$_____
Sharing Plans	$_____	$_____	$_____
Common Stock	$_____	$_____	$_____
Bonds—All Types	$_____	$_____	$_____
Real Estate	$_____	$_____	$_____
Mutual Funds	$_____	$_____	$_____
Mortgages On	$_____	$_____	$_____
Property That Needs Paid Off	$_____	$_____	$_____
Other	$_____	$_____	$_____
Total	$_____	$_____	$_____

Ⓐ Life insurance proceeds are included in the estate of the "owner" of the policy.

Ⓑ If property is jointly owned, assume that 50% of the value is owned by each spouse.

Worksheet 23-1 Estimating the Size of Your Estate

With a will there is a number of instructions you can leave regarding your property. You are allowed to leave various amounts of money and property to whomever you choose. According to the laws of intestacy, your spouse is not entitled to the complete estate. If you want your spouse to inherit everything as most people do, then you must specify these instructions in your will.

Benefits of a Will

- With a will you can give specific items to specific people. If you have a special ring you would like to leave to your niece, this is where you would do it.
- You can provide your funeral and burial instructions.
- You can name the executor of your estate.
- You can donate your body to a foundation or university for research.
- You can name the guardian for your minor children.
- You can give specific instructions on dividing your personal property.

There are two types of wills: **witnessed** and **holographic.** A witnessed will requires you to have two adults witness the signing of your will. This type of will is recognized by most states. A holographic will is one you write by hand and sign without witnesses. Few states accept holographic wills. Your probate court can tell you whether your estate allows holographic wills.

Divorced Parents

In many states a divorce will revoke your will. You should make a new will as soon as you separate and be sure to include your children. Your divorce decree can require that your ex-spouse maintains a will and makes provision for the children. You can also require that your ex-spouse set up a trust or keep the insurance in force with the children as the beneficiaries. If you don't trust your ex-spouse, have the insurance transferred to you and pay the premium yourself.

Do I Need an Attorney to Draft My Will?

Recently there has been an influx of ''do it yourself'' legal guidebooks in the bookstores for people who want to save legal fees. If you are a newcomer to the financial arena, it is recommended that you hire a good estate planning attorney. She can advise you on your state's laws and avoid costly problems that you might create by making your own will.

The cost of a will can vary from $100 for a simple document to $1,000 for a more complex estate. Complications mean extra work for your attorney who usually bills by the hour. You can save yourself money by supplying her with a list of your assets, the name of your executor, guardian for your children and instructions on how you want your estate to be distributed. Have your attorney keep the original signed copies of your will in her safe. Keep copies for yourself in your home files.

Reviewing and Updating Your Will

It is important that you keep your will current. You should review it whenever there is a major change in your life, such as a marriage, divorce, birth or a death in your family. You should also review it if there has been a substantial change in the value of your assets such as the addition of a large amount of money or property, or a change in the tax laws. If there are no changes you should still review your will every year or so to make certain it still says what you want it to say.

If you need to make a change do not mark on the original. It is not legal and can invalidate your will. Contact your attorney who will write an amendment called a "codicil," or if need be write a new will.

Probate—What Is It?

When you die, whether with a will or not, there are administrative procedures that must be completed with your estate. Someone must pay your taxes, debts and funeral expenses and supervise the distribution of your assets to your beneficiaries or heirs. It is the responsibility of the probate court to administer your estate and to make sure that the

instructions left by you in your will are properly executed.

Some of the probate procedures include transferring the title of property held in your name into the name of someone else and filing the federal and state tax forms which are required by law.

Property that Avoids Probate

Not all property in your estate needs to be probated. Property that is excluded includes that held in joint tenancy with right of survivorship, or tenancy by the entirety, your spouse's one half of the community property, property held in a living trust and life insurance and retirement plan proceeds. Property held in single name only or any share of property you hold with other persons may need to be probated.

Personal property such as furnitue and clothing which has no recorded title can usually be settled by the family rather than by probate court. If the property has a recorded title such as a car, house or land, probate is needed to transfer title into the names of your beneficiaries or heirs.

Small Estates

If you have an estate with assets of less than $30,000, many states have a small estates department which will take care of the administrative task. An executor or an attorney is generally not needed. Your state's probate court can tell you whether there is any charge for their service.

Advantages and Disadvantages of Probate

Advantages:

- Court supervision: Everyone receives what they are entitled to according to your will or under the laws of the state.
- Once the estate is probated and its assets are distributed, creditors cannot make claim against the assets.
- Probate clears titled property out of your name into the name of your beneficiaries or heirs.

Disadvantages:

- Probate is expensive: the fees are set by law and vary from state to state. It may be a fixed or sliding percentage of your probate estate. A good "ballpark" figure is 5% of your estate.
- Probate is very time consuming. It takes at least a year to probate a simple estate and longer if it more complex. The average probate time is 1½ years. During this time your heirs and beneficiaries cannot touch the assets.
- With probate your estate becomes public record. The general public and unknown creditors can obtain a copy of your will and other papers to review and make claim against your estate.

The disadvantages far outweigh the advantages and therefore it is highly recommened that you avoid probate.

How to Avoid Probate

The best method to avoid probate is by establishing an estate planning tool called the living trust which is written while you are alive and it allows your property to avoid probate and pass directly to the person you named in the trust agreement.

The two types of living trust are: **revocable** and **irrevocable.** A revocable living trust lets you receive the income from the trust while you are alive and upon your death the property passes to the trust's beneficiaries without going through probate. You can revoke the trust and take back the property at any time while you are alive.

An irrevocable trust cannot be altered or revoked. You cannot take back the property or receive any interest money. Essentially, you are making a gift to the person you name in the agreement. Because of this provision, you may not be taxed on its income during your life and you may not have to pay federal and inheritance taxes.

All types of property from personal belongings to real property can be placed into a trust. To determine whether you need a trust and what type is best for you, consult with your estate planning attorney. Expect to pay $800 or more for the drafting of a trust.

The second way to avoid probate is by

having property held in joint tenancy or tenancy by the entirety. The advantages are that it is easy to arrange and at the death of all joint tenants but the last one, the property immediately passes to the remaining tenant without going through probate. The disadvantage of joint tenancy is that property can land in the hands of beneficiaries you may not want, particularly if there is a second marriage and stepchildren are involved. Discuss this further with your attorney, financial planner or tax advisor.

Taxes: Federal and State Inheritance

Federal Estate Tax

Estate taxes are the most expensive taxes you will ever have to pay. The federal estate tax has graduated rates ranging from 40-55%. The more you have, the higher the tax rate. This is money you have earned and should be passed on to your heirs instead of to the federal government.

If you are married, the federal government currently allows you to leave your spouse all of your property tax free. There isn't a dollar limit on the size of the assets. If you leave property to anyone other than your spouse, such as your children, there is a tax-free limit of $600,000.

There are a number of methods you can use to reduce your federal estate taxes: the marital deduction, using a bypass trust, making a gift of up to $10,000 to each child or anyone else you desire every year, and giving away your life insurance by placing the proceeds into a trust. This area of discussion is much more complicated and the tax laws on federal estate taxes are always changing. Before you make any changes in your will or financial plan consult with a professional tax advisor.

State Inheritance Tax

The state inheritance tax is usually a lot less than the federal estate tax. Each state is different and bases the amount you owe individually. There isn't a $600,000 exemption as under the federal estate tax. Each beneficiary receives a separate exemption. To find out more information on the state inheritance tax in your area, contact your attorney or call your state's department of taxation.

Putting It All Together

Estate planning is an important part of your wealth building and preserving program. Its primary purpose is to pass your wealth on to your heirs while reducing the tax liabilities and saving them the burden of making wrong decisions after your death. Consult with an estate planning attorney today to draft a will and to discuss the estate saving strategies outlined in this chapter.

■ NOTES

CHAPTER 25

FINDING FINANCIAL HELP

Selecting Your Financial Advisor

Achieving financial independence is a demanding task that requires a strategic plan of action. It is very difficult to become financially independent on your own unless you can devote 100% of your time to managing your money, which most of us cannot afford to do. You will need the help of a financial, legal, and tax specialist.

Your financial advisor should be someone who shares similar views about money and financial risk taking, and puts your financial needs and goals first. She should also have the ability to communicate with you in a way that helps you understand the complexities of the various types of investments.

When selecting a financial advisor, get the names of 3 professionals. Start by asking your friends and family for advisors they would recommend. Attend financial planning and investment seminars offered in your community. This will enable you to evaluate the advisor first hand. You can also contact professional associations for recommendations.

Before making a final decision, contact the potential advisor by telephone. Explain to her that you are looking for financial assistance and ask if they would be willing to spend a few minutes with you. If so, make an appointment. They should be willing to see you for a few minutes without charge. If they insist upon charging you for the initial interview, look for someone else.

You do not want to select an advisor by pulling the name out of the yellow pages or by calling or walking into a brokerage office cold. If you do, you will most likely obtain the duty broker who may not have much experience. Instead, ask to speak to the branch manager. Discuss your financial goals and ask him to recommend 2 to 3 brokers who share investment goals similar to yours. Interview the brokers and select the one you feel the most comfortable with. You want someone whom you can easily ask questions and who will not pressure you into making an investment.

Types of Financial Advisors

Financial planners and stockbrokers are the 2 financial advisors you will encounter in developing your investment plan. A stock-broker buys and sells securities (stocks, bonds) and provides financial advice. A financial planner provides the same services and possibly more. Some financial planners have after their name the initials CFP, indicating Certified Financial Planner, a designation given to an individual who has completed 2 years of study and exams at the College of Financial Planning.

The Certified Financial Planner is knowledgeable in retirement, estate, tax, investment and business planning. She does not take the place of your attorney or accountant but works with them to help you reach your financial goals. Beware, for not all financial planners are certified. They are certified only if they have completed the above mentioned program. Verify their credentials.

Since the financial planning industry is currently not regulated you may find many people calling themselves financial planners, particularly in the insurance and financial brokerage industry. Before making a decision, interview the individual and ask questions about their investment objectives and background. The individual you select will play an important part in helping you reach your goal of financial independence.

How Financial Advisors Are Paid

There are 3 methods by which financial advisors are paid 1) fee only, 2) fee plus commission and 3) commission only.

Fee Only

A fee only advisor will analyze and provide a written comprehensive financial plan. She will make investment recommendations but will not implement them. The fee will vary with the amount of your income and assets. Most fee only advisors charge by the hour and receive no commission. When you receive their recommendations you are free to take it to either a discount or full-service brokerage firm, whichever you choose to purchase the securities. If you just want to make the transaction you should consider the discount brokerage firm, where the commission charges are lower. If you want to receive more information on the investments, contact a full-service brokerage firm.

Fee Plus Commission

The fee plus commission advisor can construct a financial plan and make recommendations on the financial products you will need to reach your goal, just as the fee only advisor.

The difference is, the fee plus commission advisor has the capacity to implement the recommendations. In return for any financial products you purchase through them, they may receive a commission. A financial plan is no good to you unless you follow through with the recommendations. If you don't have the time to devote exclusively to your finances, you are a candidate for a fee plus commission advisor.

Commission Only

The commission only advisor and stockbroker will make recommendations, but will not charge for the advice. If you follow through with their recommendations they will receive a portion of the commission. If you do not act, they will not receive compensation regardless of the time and advice they have given you.

CHAPTER 26

MILLIONAIRE POWER— STEPS TO MASTERING YOUR FINANCIAL FUTURE

The twenty-first century will place challenging financial and economic demands on the African-American community. It is imperative that you now take responsibility and equip yourself with knowledge to get your financial house in order. Knowledge is power.

As black women we can play a vital part in uplifting the welfare of the black family. Stop believing that money is the root of all evil. It is **not** having money that is currently causing havoc in the African-American community.

Money provides economic power. It gives you options in life that you otherwise would not have. If the black community exercised its economic power fully it could influence and control what books are published and read by our children, the types of movies and television programs that are produced and shown and we could start businesses that would create jobs for our unemployed men, women, and youth. In a nutshell, we could control our own financial destiny.

The advancements in telecommunications and high technology have created a global marketplace of investment opportunities. In order to take advantage of these opportunities you must obtain the financial know-how and have a solid financial plan. Take advantage of the investment classes and seminars that are offered by organizations and community colleges.

During the beginning stages of your road to financial independence it may seem that the money you are saving isn't adding up to much. But don't despair. With the magic of compounding and dollar cost averaging your small deposits can turn into a substantial amount of money. Becoming financially independent isn't easy and you will make mistakes but you will also learn from them.

If you diversify your investment portfolio and continue to ask questions you can minimize your losses and maximize your ability to be a knowledgeable investor. You will never get ahead unless you take the responsibility and invest for your future.

The following is a summary of 20 steps you must take to succeed in becoming financially independent. **GO FOR IT!** and keep your eye on the goal!
GOOD LUCK!

20 Steps to Financial Independence

- Develop a winning and positive attitude.
- Write out your financial goals, plan, and stick to them.
- Live within or below your means.
- Pay yourself first and save 10-15% of your monthly income.
- Budget monthly.
- Build and maintain an emergency cash reserve fund.
- Check your insurance needs: under insuring can cost you a lot more in the long run.
- Establish and maintain a good credit record.
- Purchase your own home.
- Reduce your taxes.
- Draft a will.
- Plan for your retirement.
- Acquire the tools and education needed to explore investment and financial opportunities.
- Teach your children about money.
- Diversify your investments and keep track of their performance.
- Maintain orderly financial records.
- Become producers not consumers.
- Start your own business and create jobs in the African-American community.
- Share your knowledge and help others to become financially independent.
- Be patient and persevere, for becoming financially independent will not happen overnight.

■ NOTES

_____

_____

_____

_____

_____

CREATE YOUR OWN FINANCIAL PLAN

Name: _____

Date: _____

Create Your Own Financial Plan

Your Name _____ Telephone No. _____

Address _____ City _____ State _____ Zip _____

Date of Birth _____ Age _____ Social Security No. _____

Spouse _____ Telephone No. _____

Address _____ City _____ State _____ Zip _____

Date of Birth _____ Age _____ Social Security No. _____

Children's Names 1)_____ 2)_____ 3)_____

Age   1)_____ 2)_____ 3)_____

Birth Date   1)_____ 2)_____ 3)_____

Social Security No. 1)_____ 2)_____ 3)_____

	You		Spouse		Combined	
Income Source	Monthly	Annually	Monthly	Annually	Monthly	Annually
1. Salary						
2. Alimony						
3. Pension						
4. Social Security						
5. Investments						
6. Other						
7. Total						

Assets

1. Checking Account, Savings Account, Credit Union, Other Cash Accounts

Name of Institution	Account No.	Interest Rate	Current Balance

2. Money Market Account, CDs, Treasury Bills and Notes.

Name of Institution	Account No.	Interest Rate	Monthly Date	Amount

3. Investment securities

Stocks and Mutual Funds:

No. of Shares	Name of Company	Date Bought	Cost	Current Value	Date Sold	Amount Sold

Bonds: Municipal—Corporate

Fare Amount	Company	Date Bought	Maturity Date	Interest Rate	Interest Income	Current Value

4. Real Estate

Location	1) _____	2) _____
Date Bought	1) _____	2) _____
Cost	1) _____	2) _____
Current Market Value	1) _____	2) _____

5. Life insurance

Company Name	1) _____	2) _____
Type of Insurance	1) _____	2) _____
Fare Amount	1) _____	2) _____
Beneficiary	1) _____	2) _____
Cash Value	1) _____	2) _____
Amount of Loan	1) _____	2) _____
Policy No.	1) _____	2) _____

6. Credit & Debt Obligations

Mortgage Holder _____

Mortgage Balance _____

Interest Rate _____

Monthly Payment _____

Loans—Auto, Education, etc.

Name of Lender	Type of Loan	Interest Rate	Balance	Monthly Date
_____	_____	_____	_____	_____
_____	_____	_____	_____	_____
_____	_____	_____	_____	_____
_____	_____	_____	_____	_____
_____	_____			

Credit Cards

Name of Card	Account Number	Balance Due
_____	_____	_____
_____	_____	_____
_____	_____	_____
_____	_____	_____

7. Individual Retirement Account, Pension, Profit Sharing Plan, Annuities.

Company Name	Description	Benefits	Current Value
_____	_____	_____	_____
_____	_____	_____	_____
_____	_____	_____	_____

Net-Worth Statement

Name: _____

Date: _____ , 19____

Assets (Has cash value)		Liabilities (Your Debts)	
Liquid Assets		**Current Debts**	
Cash and Checking Account	$_____	Rent/Mortgage	$_____
Money Market Account	$_____	Charge Accounts	$_____
CDs and Savings Account	$_____	Insurance Premiums	$_____
Stocks and Mutual Funds	$_____	Education	$_____
Bonds	$_____	Other	$_____
Cash Surrender Value Life Insurance	$_____	Total	$_____
Other	$_____	**Taxes**	
Total Liquidation Assets	$_____	Federal	$_____
Investment Assets		State	$_____
Real Estate	$_____	Property Taxes	$_____
IRA/Keogh	$_____	Social Security	$_____
Business Ownership Interest	$_____	Total	$_____
Annuities	$_____	**Other Loans**	
Notes Receivable (*money owed to you*)	$_____	Auto	$_____
Collectibles	$_____	Education	$_____
Tax Shelters	$_____	Life Insurance	$_____
Vested Pension	$_____	Home Improvement	$_____
Home Mortgage	$_____	Other	$_____
Total Investment Assets	$_____	Total	$_____
Personal Assets			
Home	$_____	**Net Worth**	
Automobile	$_____	Assets	$_____
Clothing/Jewelry etc.	$_____	Less Liabilities	–$_____
Household Goods	$_____	**Net Worth** (assets minus liabilities)	$_____
Other	$_____		
Total Assets	$_____		

Professional Contacts

	Name	Address	Telephone No.
Accountant			
Stock Broker			
Financial Planner			
Banker			
Insurance Agent			
Physician			
Attorney			
Other			

Portfolio Suggestions

Amount to Spend	In Twenties	Thirties with Children	Fifties	Retired
$1,000	Aggressive Stock Mutual Fund	Conservative Stock Mutual Fund	Conservative Growth and Income Stock Mutual Fund	U.S. Government Securities and Certificates of Deposit
$10,000	a. Down Payment on House b. IRA's $4,000 c. U.S. Government Securities d. Stock Mutual Fund e. Stocks	a. Mutual Fund for children's education b. Conservative Stock Mutual Fund c. International Mutual Funds	a. Municipal Bonds b. International Mutual Funds c. Tax-deferred Annuities	a. Bank Certificate of Deposit b. Municipal Bonds c. Corporate Bonds
$25,000	a. 10,000 Down on House b. Growth Stocks c. Stock Mutual Funds	a. Tax-deferred Annuity b. International Mutual Funds c. Blue Chip Growth Stocks	a. Real Estate b. Annuities c. International Mutual Funds	a. Bank Certificates of Deposit b. Treasury Bills c. Utility Stocks d. Corporate Bonds

Get out of Debt Fast

	Credit Cards						
Starting Date							
Total Balance Due							
Interest Rate							
January							
Amount Paid							
Interest/Penalty							
Balance Due							
February							
Amount Paid							
Interest/Penalty							
Balance Due							
March							
Amount Paid							
Interest/Penalty							
Balance Due							
April							
Amount Paid							
Interest/Penalty							
Balance Due							
May							
Amount Paid							
Interest/Penalty							
Balance Due							
June							
Amount Paid							
Interest/Penalty							
Balance Due							
July							
Amount Paid							
Interest/Penalty							
Balance Due							
August							
Amount Paid							
Interest/Penalty							
Balance Due							
September							
Amount Paid							
Interest/Penalty							
Balance Due							
October							
Amount Paid							
Interest/Penalty							
Balance Due							
November							
Amount Paid							
Interest/Penalty							
Balance Due							
December							
Amount Paid							
Interest/Penalty							
Balance Due							

Worksheet 8-3 Get out of Debt Fast

RESOURCES

■ CHILDREN & EDUCATION

Tuition Savings Program

College Savings Bank
5 Vaughn Drive
Princeton, NJ 08540-6313
(800) 888-2723

Fidelity College Savings Plan
Fidelty Investments
P. O. Box 193
Boston, MA 02101-0193
(800) 544-6666

Merrill Lynch College Builder Program
Contact your local Merrill Lynch branch
office

Scholarships & Financial Aid

Alpha Kappa Alpha Sorority, Inc.
5656 S. Stony Island Avenue
Chicago, IL 60637
(312) 684-1282

American Fund for Dental Health
Fellowships
211 East Chicago Avenue
Chicago, IL 60611

American Institute of Certified Public
Accountants
1211 Avenue of the Americas
New York, NY 10036
(800) 862-4272

Chi Eta Phi Sorority, Inc.
3029 13th Street, NW
Washington, DC 20009
(202) 723-3384
(nursing scholarships)

Delta Sigma Theta Sorority, Inc.
1707 New Hampshire Avenue, NW
Washington, DC 20009
(202) 483-5460

Links, Inc.
1200 Massachusetts Avenue, NW
Washington, DC 20003
(202) 842-8696
(scholarships for artists)

NAACP Legal Defense &
Educational Fund, Inc.
99 Hudson Street, Suite 1600
New York, NY 10013
(212) 219-1900

National Action Council for Minorities in
Engineering
3 West 35th Street
New York, NY 10001
(212) 279-2626 (phone)
(212) 629-5178 (fax)

National Black Nurses Association, Inc.
1012 10th Street, NW
Washington, DC 20001
(202) 393-6870

National Medical Fellowships, Inc.
254 West 31st Street 7th Floor
New York, NY 10001
(212) 741-0933

United Negro College Fund, Inc.
500 East 62nd Street
New York, NY 10021
(212) 326-1118

Other Resources & Programs

American Bankers Association
The Personal Economics Program
1120 Connecticut Avenue, NW
Washington, DC 20036
(202) 663-5394

Children's Financial Network
252 West 85th Street, Apt. 8A
New York, NY 10024
(212) 683-8676

Dollars & Sense Financial Camp
Smart Services, Inc.
255 Sunrise Avenue
Palm Beach, FL 33480
(407) 655-2229

Illinois State Treasurer's Office
Bank-at-School Program
James R. Thompson Office Building
100 West Randolph
Suite 15-600
Chicago, IL 60601
(312) 814-1700
(teaches school children basic banking skills)

Inroads Inc.
1221 Locust Street, Suite 800
St. Louis, MO 63103
(314) 241-7488
(mentoring program)

Junior Achievement, Inc.
45 Clubhouse Drive
Colorado Springs, CO 80906
(719) 540-9000

National Center for Financial Education
P. O. Box 3914
San Diego, CA 92163
(619) 232-8811

Oakland Youth Corporation
262 Grand Avenue, Suites 200 & 205
Oakland, CA 94610
(510) 465-5999

Young Investors Mutual Fund
Stein Roe & Farnham
1330 Avenue of the Americas
New York, NY 10036
(212) 489-0131

Young American Education Foundation
Young American Bank
250 Steele Street
Denver, CO 80206
(303) 321-2954

Youth Organizations USA
19 Humprey Street
Englewood, NJ 07631
(201) 836-1838

■ INVESTMENTS

Mutual Funds

Berger Funds
Berger Associates
P. O. Box 5005
Denver, CO 80217
(800) 333-1001

Morningstar Mutual Fund Newsletter
225 West Wacker Drive
Floor 4
Chicago, IL 60606
(312) 696-6000

Twentieth Century Investors
P. O. Box 200
Kansas City, MO 64141
(800) 345-2021

Socially Reponsible Investment Funds

These mutual funds only buy securities that meet certain ethnical standards. Before investing, call or write for a current prospectus.

Calvert-Ariel Growth Fund
1700 Pennsylvania Avenue, NW
Washington, DC 20006
(800) 368-2748

Calvert Social Investment Fund
1700 Pennsylvania Avenue, NW
Washington, DC 20006
(800) 368-2748

Dreyfus Third Century Fund
600 Madison Avenue
New York, NY 10022
(800) 546-6561

American Association of Individual Investors
Corporation
625 North Michigan Avenue
Suite 1900
Chicago, IL 60611
(312) 280-0170

Pax World Fund
224 State Street
Portsmouth, NH 03801
(800) 343-0529

Pioneer Three Fund
Box 9014
Boston, MA 02205
(800) 225-6292

Standard & Poor's Corporation
Financial Services Department
25 Broadway
New York, NY 10004
(212) 208-8000

Value Line Funds
220 East 42nd Street
New York, NY 10017
(212) 907-1500

Working Assets Money Fund
230 California Street
San Francisco, CA 94111
(800) 543-8800

Mutual Funds Families with Global/ International Funds

Calvert New Africa Fund
New Africa Advisors
4550 Montgomery Avenue
Bethesda, MD 20814
(800) 368-2750

Fidelity Investments
P. O. Box 193
Boston, MA 02101-0193
(800) 544-6666

G. T. Global Financial Services
Fifty California Street, 27th Floor
San Francisco, CA 94111
(800) 824-1580

Templeton International
700 Central Avenue
St. Petersburg, FL 33733
(800) 237-0738

T. Rowe Price Investment Services, Inc.
100 East Pratt Street
Baltimore, MD 21202
(800) 638-5660

Discount Brokerages

Charles Schwab & Co. Inc.
101 Montgomery Street
San Francisco, CA 94104
(415) 398-1000

Charles Schwab & Co. Inc.
One World Trade Center
New York, NY 10047
(212) 938-0404

Investment Clubs

National Association of Investment Clubs
1515 East Eleven Mile Road
Royal Oak, MI 48067
(810) 583-6242

■ DEBT MANAGEMENT

Credit Cards

Debt Zapper Kit
Bankcard Holders of America
524 Branch Drive
Salem, VA 24153
(703) 389-5445
(also available, lists of bank cards with low
interest or no annual fee)

Debtors Anonymous
(Meetings are held in cities nationwide;
check your local white pages for listing)

National Foundation for Consumer Credit
88701 Georgia Avenue, Suite 507
Silver Springs, MD 20901
(800) 388-2227

Credit Rating Agencies

TRW
505 City Parkway West
Orange, CA 92668
(714) 385-7000

Credit Rating Bureau, Inc. (CBF)
P. O. Box 95007
Atlanta, GA 30347
(404) 252-9559

■ RETIREMENT & PENSIONS

American Association of Retired Persons
(AARP)
601 E Street, NW
Washington, DC 20049
(800) 424-3410

National Center for Women and Retirement
Research
Long Island University
Southampton Campus
Southampton, NY 11968
(800) 426-7386
(Provides books and seminars on retirement
to women nationwide)

Social Security Administration
Washington, DC 20402
(to request your earnings and benefit estimate
statement; you can also contact your local
Social Security office)

T. Rowe Price Retirement Planning Kit
T. Rowe Price Investment Services, Inc.
100 East Pratt Street
Baltimore, MD 21202
(800) 638-5660

■ HIGH-TECH MONEY MANAGEMENT

Software

Quicken Personal Finance
(800) 624-9060

Managing Your Money
(800) 537-9993

Microsoft Money
(800) 434-3976

Kiplinger's Simply Money
(800) 773-5445

Your Mutual Fund Selector
Intuit Software
(800) 624-6930

Electronic Bill Paying

Checkfree Corporation
P. O. Box 897
Columbus, OH 43272
(800) 882-5280

RECOMMENDED READING

Books

Beckham, Barry, ed. *The Black Student's Guide to Colleges: Profiles of 182 Colleges, Black and White*. Beckham House Publishers, 1995.

Berryessa, Norman, and Eric Kirzner. *Global Investing: The Templeton Way*. Irwin Professional Publishing, 1988.

Bohigian, Valerie. *Ladybucks: Why Certain Women Turn Work into Wealth*. Valian Associates, 1987.

Clason, George S. *The Richest Man in Babylon: The Success Secrets of the Ancients*. NAL/Dutton, 1988.

Clifford, Denis, and Cora Jordan. *Plan Your Estate: Wills, Probate Avoidance, Trusts, and Taxes*. Nolo Press, 1989.

Feldman, Beverly Never. *Kids Who Succeed: The No-Nonsense Guide to Raising a Child Who'll be a Winner in Tomorrow's World*. Fawcett Crest, 1987.

Graham, Benjamin. *The Intelligent Investor*. HarperCollins, 1973.

Hill, Napoleon. *Think and Grow Rich*. Fawcett Books, 1987.

Kinder, Peter, Amy L. Domini, and Steven D. Lydenberg. *Investing for Good: Making Money while being Socially Responsible*. HarperCollins, 1994.

Kunjufu, Jawanza. *Motivating and Preparing Black Youth to Work*. (African American Images, 1986.

Landry, Bart. *The New Black Middle Class*. University of California Press, 1987.

Lynch, Peter, with John Rothschild. *One Up on Wall Street: How to Use What You Already Know to Make Money in the Market*. Penguin Books, 1989.

Moskowitz, Milton. *The Global Marketplace: 102 of the Most Influential Companies Outside America*. Macmillan, 1987.

Ponder, Catherine. *The Dynamic Laws of Prosperity: Forces that Bring Riches to You*. DeVorss Co., 1985.

Ross, Ruth. *Prospering Woman: A Complete Guide to Achieving the Full Abundant Life*. Bantam Books, 1985.

Sanaya, Roman, and Duane Packer. *Creating Money: Keys to Abundance*. H. J. Kramer, Inc., 1988.

Schwartz, David J. *The Magic of Thinking Success: Your Personal Guide to Financial Independence* (Wilshire Book Co., 1987.

Sidel, Ruth. *Women and Children Last: The Plight of Poor Women in Affluent America*. Penguin Books, 1987.

Trower-Subira, George. *Black Folks' Guide to Making Big Money in America*. Very Serious Business Enterprises, 1980.

Warfield, Gerald. *How to Buy Foreign Stocks and Bonds*. HarperCollins, 1985.

Woodhouse, Violet and Victoria Felton-Collins, with M.C. Blakeman. *Divorce & Money: How to Make the Best Financial*

Decisions During Divorce. Nolo Press, 1993.

Booklets & Directories

Directory of Financial Aids for Minorities. Gail Ann Schlachter and R. David Weber. Reference Service Press, 1100 Industrial Road, San Carlos, CA 94070.

Directory of Financial Aids for Women. Gail Ann Schlachter and R. David Weber. Reference Service Press, 1100 Industrial Road, San Carlos, CA 94070.

A Guide to Understanding Your Pension Plan (D13533). AARP, 601 E Street, NW, Washington, DC 20049. (800) 424-3410.

Higher Education Opportunities for Minorities and Women. Government Printing Office.

How to Start an Investment Club. Washington Women's Investment Club, P. O. Box 3763, Washington, DC 20007.

Protect Yourself: A Woman's Guide to Pension Rights (D12258). AARP, 601 E Street, NW, Washington, DC 20049. (800) 424-3410.

You and Money. Fidelity Investments, P. O. Box 193, Boston, MA 02101-0193. (800) 544-6666

Reading for Children

Barbanel, Linda. *Piggy Bank to Credit Cards: Teach Your Child the Financial Facts of Life.* Crown Publishers, 1994.

Bodnar, Janet. *Kiplinger's Money-Smart Kids —and Parents Too.* Kiplinger Books, 1993.

Drew, Bonnie. *Money Skills: 101 Activities to Teach Your Child About Money.* Career Press, 1992.

Peterson, Jean R. *It Doesn't Grow on Trees.* Betterway Books, 1988.

Smith, Allan. *Teenage Money Making Guide.* Success Publishing, 1984.

Magazines

Black Enterprise
Ebony
Emerge
Entrepreneurial Woman
Essence
Forbes
Fortune
Kiplinger Personal Finance
Money Magazine
Smart Money
Your Future (special edition of *Money Magazine*)

Newspapers

Barrons
Financial Times (London)
Investors Daily
Los Angeles Times
The New York Times
USA Today
The Wall Street Journal

"Oakland Students Urged to Set Goals to Succeed" (interview with Reginald Lewis). *Oakland Tribune*, April 9, 1995.

Accrued dividend. When a dividend is earned but not declared or payable, it is added to the value of the asset.

Accrued interest. Interest accrued on a bond since the last interest payment was made. The buyer of the bond pays the market price plus accrued interest.

Accumulation plan. A plan in which mutual fund shares are purchased through periodic investment and reinvestment of income dividends and capital gain distribution.

Adjustable rate mortgage (ARM). A mortgage whose interest rate is tied to a floating index rate, such as U.S. Treasury bills.

Adjusted gross income (AGI). The calculation of your personal tax liability minus adjustments for payments made to an individual retirement account (IRA), and business expenses. Itemized and standard deductions, charitable contributions and personal exemptions are not included.

Alternative minimum tax (AMT). A device used by the IRS to make sure that wealthy individuals, trusts, and estates are not able to escape from tax liabilities through tax preference strategies.

American depository receipt (ADR). A security sold by banks allowing investors to invest in foreign securities without the usual delays and currency rate fluctuations.

Amex. The American Stock Exchange located in New York City.

Amortizations. A plan used to reduce a debt gradually through scheduled payments. Also an accounting method by which the price of an asset is reduced over time to reflect it's declining resale value.

Annual percentage rate (APR). The interest rate applied to a loan.

Annual report. A year end financial statement issued yearly by the corporation. The annual report shows assets, liabilities, income statements, and other information of interest to shareowners.

Annuity. A contract with an insurance company with a series of payments measured in terms of a warranted number of years.

Appreciation. The amount of increase in value of an asset.

Arbitrage. A technique of buying and selling commodities in 2 separate markets to take advantage of difference in price.

Ask price. The lowest price at which a security is offered for sale.

Asset. An item that is owned.

Auction market. The system of trading securities through brokers or agents on an exchange such as the New York Stock Exchange.

Audit. An examination of financial documents by an independent accountant for adherence to legal and accounting principles.

Averages. Various ways of measuring the trend of securities prices, one of the most popular is the Dow-Jones average of 30 industrial stocks listed on the New York Stock Exchange.

Back-end load. A sales charge paid when an asset is sold or transferred.

Balance sheet. A condensed financial statement showing the nature and amount of a company; assets, liabilities, and capital on a certain date.

Balanced fund. A fund that earns both current income and capital gains.

Bankruptcy. The inability of a company or individual to pay debts as determined by a federal court.

Bear market. A declining stock market.

Bearer bond. A bond that does not have the owner's name registerd on the book of the issuer and is payable to the holder.

Beneficiaries. The designated recipients of insurance policy proceeds.

Bid price. The highest price offered to purchase a given security.

Big board. A term for the New York Stock Exchange.

Blue chip stock. A stock known for its quality and having a stable record of earnings and dividends.

Bond. An IOU or promissory note of a corporation who agrees to pay a stated rate of interest over a specified period of time, at the end of which the original sum will be returned.

Bond fund. A mutual fund that deals exclusively in bonds and primarily seeks income with capital gains as a secondary objective.

Bond yield. An annual rate of return that an investor would receive on a bond if it were held to maturity.

Book value. The amount of shareholder's equity in any firm derived by subtracting liabilities and preferred stocks from assets held.

Coupon bond. Bond with interest coupons attached. The coupons are clipped as they come due and are presented by the holder for payment of interest.

Cumulative preferred. A stock with a provision that if 1 or more dividends are omitted, the omitted dividend must be paid before dividends on common stock can be paid.

Custodian. A corporation such as a bank or an individual charged with the safekeeping of a company's investment portfolio.

Dealer. An individual or firm in the securities business acting as a principal rather than as an agent. A dealer usually buys for his own account and sells to individuals.

Debenture. A promissory note backed by the general credit of a company and usually not secured by a mortgage or lien on any specific property.

Debt balance. The amount of money being borrowed or the size of the margin loan.

Debt-Equity ratio. A measure of what is owed and what is owned.

Deferred annuity. An annuity where benefits are scheduled to begin sometime in the future at a specific date.

Depreciation. Changes against earnings to write off the cost, less salvage value of an asset over its useful life. It is a bookkeeping entry and does not represent any cash outlay.

Depression. An extended recession in the business cycle. Prices fall, unemployment rises, production declines, and business activity in general declines.

Deficit. The amount by which total expenses exceed total income.

Disability insurance. Insurance that provides periodic payments to replace income when the insured is unable to work due to a covered injury or illness.

Discount bond. Bonds with a market value lower than par.

Discount broker. Brokers who make securities transactions at lower commissions for customers not needing advice or services that are regularly offered at full service brokerage firms.

Discretionary account. An account in which the customer gives the broker or someone else discretion to purchase or sell securities.

Diversification. Spreading investment dollars

into a variety of investment vehicles for the purpose of reducing risk.

Dividend. A payment made by a corporation to shareholders.

Dividend reinvestment plan. Plan that allows shareholders to reinvest their dividend into additional shares of common stock.

Dollar cost averaging. A system of buying securities at regular intervals with a fixed dollar amount.

Dow Jones Industrial Average (DJIA). The Dow Jones Company publishes 4 stock indicators daily. The Dow Jones Industrial Average follows the value of 30 leading industrial stocks; the Dow Jones Transportation Average (DJTA) tracks 20 airline, railroad, and trucking stocks. The Dow Jones Utility Average (DJUA) monitors 15 gas and electric utility stocks and the "Dow 65," the composite combines all three.

Down payment. The money buyers must put up as a minimum to secure a property.

Earnings per share (EPS). The net earnings of a corporation divided by the number of outstanding shares of common stock.

EE bonds. U.S. government savings bonds sold at 50% discount from face value and redeemed in full in 11 years.

Equity. An ownership interest in a specific business or property.

Estate planning. The strategy for protecting your assets at death. Includes writing a will.

Euro dollars. U.S. currency that is held in foreign banks.

Executor. The person named in a will to carry out the wishes of the deceased.

Face value. The value of a bond that appears on the face of the bond. The issuer guarantees to repay the lender the face value of the obligation at maturity.

Federal Deposit Insurance Corporation.
(FDIC). The federal agency that insures deposits of up to $100,000 in member banks.

Federal Housing Administration (FHA). A federally sponsored agency that insures leaders against losses on residential mortgage lending.

Federal Savings and Loan Insurance Corp. (FSLIC). The federal agency that insures the deposits in member savings and loan organizations.

Fixed expenses. Household expenses that do not vary from month to month.

401(k) plan. A profit sharing plan for employees. They are allowed to reduce their income by investing a portion which is matched by the employer. The earnings grow tax free and the employee contributions are excluded from federal income tax.

Floor. The trading area of a stock exchange where stocks and bonds are bought and sold.

Global Fund. A mutual fund that invests in U.S. and foreign stocks.

Good till canceled order (GTC). An order to buy or sell which remains in effect until it is executed or cancelled.

Government National Mortgage Association (Ginnie Mae or GNMA). A government agency that purchases mortgages from private lenders. The mortgages are repackaged and sold as mortgage-backed securities on the open market.

Gross national product (GNP). The market value of all goods and services produced by a country over the period of a year.

Holographic will. A hand-written will. They are valid only in some states.

Income property. Residential, commercial, or industrial property that provides rental income to its owner.

Income statement. A summary of the total income and expenses of an individual or organization.

Individual Retirement Account (IRA). A retirement savings program that allows individuals to make tax deductible contributions. Earnings are not taxed until the funds are withdrawn.

Inflation. An economic condition of rising prices attributed to the over expansion of the money supply.

Inflation hedge. An asset that appreciates in value at a rate equal to or exceeding the rate of inflation.

Initial public offering (IPO). A corporation's first stock offering to the public.

Insider trading. Illegal securities trading based on information not available to the general public.

Inter-Vivos trust (living trust). A trust formed during the grantor's lifetime.

Interest. Payments made by the borrower to a lender for the use of the money.

Intestate. When a decedent does not leave a will, leaving disbursement of the property up to the state.

Irrevocable trust. The grantor gives away all rights of ownership and which cannot be revoked.

Joint Tenancy. Ownership of property by 2 or more people.

Junk Bond. A bond rated BB or lower by an investment rating service. Junk bonds are riskier and pay above average yields.

Keogh plan. A retirement savings plan for self-employed individuals.

Leverage. The use of borrowed money for investment purposes.

Leveraged buy out (LBO). The takeover of a company using borrowed money.

Liabilities. Debts currently outstanding.

Liability insurance. Insurance that provides protection against the risk that the insured might cause property damage or bodily injury to some-one else. Usually included as part of home owner's and automobile insurance policies.

Lien. A claim against property.

Limit order. An order to buy or sell at specific price.

Limited partnership. A form of business organization where small investors (limited partners) pool their funds and participate in programs that are regularly available only to wealthy investors. Limited partners liability is limited to their investment.

Liquidity. The ability to quickly convert an investment to cash.

Listed stock. The stock of a company that is traded on an exchange.

Load fund. A mutual fund that charges a sales charge to buy or sell.

Lump-sum distribution. One time disbursement of the proceeds of a profit sharing or pension plan.

Margin. The amount paid by the customer when they use the broker's credit to buy a security.

Market order. An order to buy or sell a stated amount of a security at the best price.

Martial deduction. Created the Economic Recovery Act of 1981. Allows the assets of one spouse to pass tax free to the other on the death of the first.

Maturity. The date on which a loan or a bond comes due and is to be paid off.

Money market. The market created for short term debt instruments such as commercial paper, banker's acceptance, and other short-term instruments.

Money market fund. A mutual fund that invests in short-term instruments.

Mortgage. A debt instrument where a borrower obtains money from a lender using the property as collateral. The borrower has use of the property and the lien is removed once the loan is paid off.

Municipal bond. A bond issued by a state, county, city, or town. Interest paid on municipal bonds is exempt from federal income taxes and state and local income taxes within the state of issue.

Mutual fund. An open-end investment company created by management in which the money of many individuals is pooled together to purchase a diversified portfolio of securities.

National Association of Securities Dealers (NASD). A self-regulatory association to oversee the brokers and dealers who operate the over-the-counter market.

National Association of Security Dealers Automated Quotation System (NASDAQ). An automated information network which provides brokers and dealers with price quotations on securities traded over-the-counter.

Net asset valve (NAV). The price at which a mutual fund redeems its share. Calculated daily by dividing the net market value of the fund divided by the number of outstanding shares.

Net worth. The ownership position or amount of wealth or equity in assets owned.

No-Load fund. A mutual fund that does not charge a sales commission.

Odd lot. A stock order of less than 100 shares.

Option. A right to bug (call) or sell (put) a fixed amount of a given stock at a specified price within a limited period of time.

Over-the-Counter Market (OTC). A market for the exchange of securities that are not listed on the organized stock exchange. Trades are conducted by telephone and over a computer network.

Par value. The stated or face value of a stock; the principal amount of a bond.

Penny stock. Low-priced stocks, many sell for less than $1. Highly speculative.

Point. In lending, the amount paid to the lender as a loan fee or 1% of principal. In stock, it means a $1 price fluctuation.

Portfolio. Holdings of securities by an individual or institution. A portfolio may contain bonds, stocks, and preferred stock.

Preferred stock. A class of stock with a claim on the company; earnings before payment may be made on the common stock.

Probate. The period of time when a court supervises the affairs of the decedent.

Prospectus. The document that must be given to purchasers of new securities registered with the Securities and Exchange Commission so investors can evaluate those securities before or at the time of purchase.

Proxy. Written authorization given by a shareholder to someone else to represent them and vote their shares at a shareholder's meeting.

Put. An option to see 100 shares of stock at a specified price within a set period of time.

Qualified retirement plan. An IRS-approved pension and profit-sharing plan established by an employer for the employees.

Quote. The highest bid to buy and the lowest offer to sell a security in a given market at a given time.

Rally. A brisk rise following a decline in the stock market or an individual stock.

Real Estate Investment Trust (REIT). A closed-end investment company that invests money in mortgages and other types of real estate.

Recession. A severe contraction in the economy.

Red herring. A preliminary prospectus used to determine interest in the offering. It is stamped in red on the prospectus.

Redeem. To sell.

Registered representative. An employee of a firm that is a member of the stock exchange who acts as an account executive to clients.

Return. Pre-tax profit on an investment.

Risk. Measurable possibility of loss or no gain on an investment.

Rollover. The transfer of retirement funds from a qualified retirement plan into a rollover IRA.

Round lot. On the NYSE, a lot of 100 shares.

Rule of 72. A formula for calculating the number of years an investment will double at a given compound interest rate.

SEC. The Securities and Exchange Commission. Established to help protect investors. It oversees investment tracing activities.

SEP-IRA. Simplified Employee Pension Plan. A qualified retirement plan where employees establish their own individual retirement accounts and the employer may make a contribution.

Standard & Poor's. An investor's service and financial publishing firm.

Short selling. The sale of stock that is not owned by the investor but has been borrowed from a broker in anticipation of a drop in the stock's value.

Stock. Ownership shares of a corporation.

Stop order. An order to buy at a price above or sell at a price below the current market.

Tax bracket. The range of taxable income taxed at a certain rate.

Tax-deferred investment. An investment where the earnings are not taxed until they are withdrawn.

Tax-exempt security. A security whose interest is exempt from federal or state taxes. Ex. Municipal Bonds.

Tax shelter. Certain investments that can lower ordinary taxable income.

Tenancy by the entirety. A form of registration of property.

Tenancy in common. Ownership of property or securities by 2 or more people, each owns a defined percentage.

Term life insurance. A life insurance policy that is issued for a limited time period specified in the contract.

Treasury bill. Short-term securities issued and backed by the U.S. government, sold in minimum denominations of $10,000. Maturities range from 13 to 52 weeks.

Treasury bond. Securities backed by the U.S. government with maturity dates that extend to 25 years or longer.

Treasury note. U.S. government securities with a maturity of not less than 1 year and not more than 10 years.

Trust. A legal entity created by an individual in which another person or institution holds and manages property for a third party.

Universal life insurance. Life insurance that consists of a term policy and a savings accumulation plan.

Unlisted. A stock not listed on a stock exchange.

V.A. mortgage. A residential mortgage that is guaranteed by the Veterans Administration.

Vesting. The time necessary for an employee to become a participant in a qualified retirement plan.

Warrant. A certificate giving the holder the right to purchase securities at a stipulated price within a specified time limit.

Whole-life insurance. Insurance coverage over the entire life of an insured.

Yield. The rate of return earned by an investment.

Zero coupon bond. A bond sold at a deep discount from its par or face value.

INDEX

FOR THE BEST IN PAPERBACKS, LOOK FOR THE

In every corner of the world, on every subject under the sun, Penguin represents quality and variety—the very best in publishing today.

For complete information about books available from Penguin—including Puffins, Penguin Classics, and Arkana—and how to order them, write to us at the appropriate address below. Please note that for copyright reasons the selection of books varies from country to country.

In the United Kingdom: Please write to *Dept. JC, Penguin Books Ltd, FREEPOST, West Drayton, Middlesex UB7 0BR.*

If you have any difficulty in obtaining a title, please send your order with the correct money, plus ten percent for postage and packaging, to *P.O. Box No. 11, West Drayton, Middlesex UB7 0BR*

In the United States: Please write to *Consumer Sales, Penguin USA, P.O. Box 999, Dept. 17109, Bergenfield, New Jersey 07621-0120.* VISA and MasterCard holders call 1-800-253-6476 to order all Penguin titles

In Canada: Please write to *Penguin Books Canada Ltd, 10 Alcorn Avenue, Suite 300, Toronto, Ontario M4V 3B2*

In Australia: Please write to *Penguin Books Australia Ltd, P.O. Box 257, Ringwood, Victoria 3134*

In New Zealand: Please write to *Penguin Books (NZ) Ltd, Private Bag 102902, North Shore Mail Centre, Auckland 10*

In India: Please write to *Penguin Books India Pvt Ltd, 706 Eros Apartments, 56 Nehru Place, New Delhi 110 019*

In the Netherlands: Please write to *Penguin Books Netherlands bv, Postbus 3507, NL-1001 AH Amsterdam*

In Germany: Please write to *Penguin Books Deutschland GmbH, Metzlerstrasse 26, 60594 Frankfurt am Main*

In Spain: Please write to *Penguin Books S. A., Bravo Murillo 19, 1° B, 28015 Madrid*

In Italy: Please write to *Penguin Italia s.r.l., Via Felice Casati 20, I-20124 Milano*

In France: Please write to *Penguin France S. A., 17 rue Lejeune, F–31000 Toulouse*

In Japan: Please write to *Penguin Books Japan, Ishikiribashi Building, 2–5–4, Suido, Bunkyo-ku, Tokyo 112*

In Greece: Please write to *Penguin Hellas Ltd, Dimocritou 3, GR–106 71 Athens*

In South Africa: Please write to *Longman Penguin Southern Africa (Pty) Ltd, Private Bag X08, Bertsham 2013*